The Literacy Center

The Literacy Center

Contexts for Reading and Writing

Lesley Mandel Morrow

Rutgers University

Stenhouse Publishers
York, Maine

Stenhouse Publishers, 431 York Street, York, Maine 03909

Credits
Pages 73, 74, 76, and 80: Lesley Mandel Morrow, "Motivating Reading and Writing in Diverse Classrooms," NCTE Research Paper No. 28. Copyright © 1996 by the National Council of Teachers of English. Reprinted with permission.

Page 154: *Harold and the Purple Crayon*. Copyright © 1955 by Crockett Johnson, copyright © renewed 1983 by Ruth Krauss.

Pages 171–174: "Stories Good Enough to Eat," from *Organizing and Managing Literacy Centers*. Copyright © 1983 Lesley Mandel Morrow. Reprinted by permission of *Instructor Magazine*, August 1983. Scholastic.

Library of Congress Cataloging-in-Publication Data
Morrow, Lesley Mandel.
      The literacy center : contexts for reading and writing / Lesley Mandel Morrow.
          p.   cm.
      Includes bibliographical references (p.).
      ISBN 1–57110–022–9 (alk. paper)
      1. Language arts (Elementary).   2. Language arts—Correlation with content subjects.   3. Classroom environment.   4. Group work in education.   5. Motivation in education.   I. Title.
      LB1576.M797   1997   96–6499
      372.6'044—dc21   CIP

Cover and interior design by Catherine Hawkes
Illustrations by Phyllis Pittet
Typeset by Octal Publishing, Inc.

Manufactured in the United States of America on acid-free paper

01 00 99   9 8 7 6 5 4

*To my mother, Mary D. Mandel, whose love, guidance,
and friendship have been so important to me, and whose
strength, wisdom, and wonderful sense of humor I have
learned to appreciate all the more in recent years.*

Contents

Resources

Acknowledgments

This book is a result of my many years of teaching children as well as pre-service and in-service teachers. It is the practical application of the research I have carried out for the past sixteen years. The ideas come from the work I have done with others involved in my teaching from kindergarten through college, and in staff development programs.

I am indebted to the hundreds of children, teachers, administrators, and parents who allowed me to teach their children and collect information to share with others. I would like particularly to thank Jerilyn Bier, Donna Fino Eng, Diane Huggard, Ami Levin, Elizabeth Minnick, Dana Pilla, and Karen Price for their work in several portions of the book. A special acknowledgment goes to Lisa Lozak for the exceptional work she did in the resource section. Without their help, I could never have completed this manuscript.

Motivating Reading and Writing: Current Research

Mrs. Johnson's third graders were participating in writing and reading appreciation program (WRAP) time. (The phrase is credited to Gloria Lettenberger, a first-grade ESL teacher in the New Brunswick public schools.) Steven, Kevin, and Rashaan were sitting on a rug in the literacy center, resting against pillows. They were looking at copies of the same issue of *Ranger Rick* magazine. Steven popped up and said to the others, "Hey, you guys. Look at all those spiders on page 22! Aren't they neat!" Kevin and Rashaan looked over at Steven's copy, then turned to the same page in theirs. The boys were engrossed as they read and talked about the spiders. "Look!" Kevin exclaimed. "It says here, spiders have eight legs. I didn't know that."

Tia, Neela, and Brian were under a shelf filled with stuffed animals. Tia was in the middle, reading to the others as they followed along, looking at the print and pictures. After listening for a while, Neela asked if she could read, and Tia handed over the book when she finished the page she was on.

Tamika and Alexis were squeezed into the same rocking chair, each of them reading her own book silently. Larry was sitting in a bean-bag chair by himself, reading a novel.

At the listening station, four children were listening to a tape of *Ming Lo Moves the Mountain* (Lobel 1982). When it was done, Jonathan said to the others, "You know, I don't think Ming Lo is very smart. He kept doing silly things just because the wise man told him to do them." The statement started a lively discussion about whether Ming Lo should have done the things the wise man told him to do without any questions.

Yassin, Michael, and Howard were in the author's spot. They were working together at the computer, writing their own episode of a favorite television show. They decided that when they completed their story they would make it into a roll movie. They could then present it to the group as if it were on television. They discussed how many pictures they

Yassin, Michael, and Howard in the author's spot. They are working together on their own episode of a favorite television show.

needed to draw for the dialogue and who would draw which ones. They decided that each of them would read the segment he had written with the accompanying illustration for the presentation to the class. They got the materials they needed and began to work.

Colleen, Shakiera, Keisha, Kelly, and Brian were practicing a puppet show they had created from the book *Arthur's Eyes* (Brown 1979). They made stick puppets and were going to present the story to the class at sharing time, which is held after WRAP time for students who want to perform or talk about the work they are doing. Mrs. Johnson sat and watched as they performed the story. She congratulated them on a job well done. Keisha asked Mrs. Johnson if she thought the characters had acted the way the author of the story would have wanted them to. Mrs. Johnson replied, "If Mr. Brown, the author of *Arthur's Eyes*, walked into our classroom right now, he would think that he had directed this puppet show. I think the characters act just as he would have wanted them to."

These children are motivated to participate in literacy activities in their classroom. Its physical and social contexts have been designed to foster independent participation that is social, collaborative, and cooperative. In this book I discuss strategies that have been successful in motivating reading and writing activities in school and at home. For many years I have been researching ways to motivate children to read and write for pleasure and for information. My work has taken me to classrooms in suburban communities and urban settings, and I have worked with children from diverse backgrounds. In applying principles of motivation to classroom practice, I have found that classrooms need to provide children with certain elements: choice, challenge, social interaction, and success.

In the pages that follow, I outline how to create rich literacy environments through the design of literacy centers in the classroom. Teachers can be seen as architects who design the environment to support strategies for learning. I describe how the teachers I've worked with model pleasurable and skill-oriented literacy activities, such as reading to children and storytelling, so that children will engage in these activities themselves. After the teacher models activities, students form groups and work together to use the materials and do the activities modeled by the teacher. They then create their own materials for books they have read and stories they have written, which they present to peers and parents.

This book is filled with practical suggestions from the teachers, children, and parents who have participated in the different programs they and I were involved in together. Activities and forms are provided to help teachers design their own literacy centers, model the materials for students, and initiate a literacy center time for children to interact with each other while engaged in literacy activities. In these settings children function in the environment with peers or alone, independent of the teacher.

Research on motivation and learning points to the need for certain physical and social elements to be present in classrooms to help motivate children. Before getting into what those elements are and how to build them into the classroom, let us briefly survey the research and theories themselves.

The Integrated Language Arts Perspective

Much attention has been focused recently on developing literacy through integrating language arts. The integrated language arts perspective is a philosophy concerning how children learn and, more specifically, how children acquire literacy. From this philosophy educators have developed strategies for teaching.

The integrated language arts perspective suggests that children learn literacy from a series of authentic, meaningful, and functional experiences with reading and writing, using varied genres of children's literature. Those experiences take place within a rich environment created specifically to encourage collaboration and cooperative learning during periods set aside for independent reading and writing. Instruction includes a conscious effort on the part of the teacher to integrate literacy learning throughout the school day within the different content areas (social studies, science, math, art, and music). Equal emphasis is placed on reading, writing, listening, oral language, and viewing because all help to create a literate individual. Skills are taught when they are relevant and meaningful; for example, when studying dinosaurs, the teacher may focus on the letters and sounds of the initial consonants found in the names of dinosaurs. The integrated language arts approach emphasizes learning that is largely self-regulated by students through their selection of materials, activities, and partners. Teachers and children together are responsible for deciding instructional strategies, organization, activities, and materials

(Bergeron 1990; Goodman 1989a; Goodman 1989b).

In designing classrooms that follow an integrated language arts perspective, educators draw a great deal from Don Holdaway (1979) and his theory of developmental learning. Holdaway placed equal emphasis on learning and teaching. Instead of just teaching lessons in literacy, for example, teachers should provide guidance and models of literacy activities for children to emulate. According to Holdaway, four processes enable children to acquire reading ability. The first is *observation* of reading behaviors—being read to, for example, or seeing adults reading. The second is *collaboration* with an individual (a teacher or peer) who interacts with the child, providing encouragement, motivation, and help when necessary. The third process is *practice*. The learner tries out alone what has been learned and experiments without adult direction. Practice gives children opportunities to evaluate their performance, make corrections, and increase their skills. In the fourth process, *performance,* the child shares what has been learned and seeks approval from adults and peers who are supportive, interested, and encouraging. There is adult and peer interaction as children observe others engaged in literacy acts, and as they interact in literacy experiences together. There is the opportunity for peer tutoring and collaboration in active literacy experiences. In classrooms such as this, projects are process oriented and may take a long period of time to complete (Holdaway 1979; Newman 1985; Wells 1985).

Thus, in an integrated language arts program, teachers provide students with the following experiences (Routman 1991):

- Reading aloud by teachers and children.

- Shared reading and writing by teachers and children.

- Teacher-guided reading and writing activities.

- Independent reading and writing activities.

- Collaborative reading and writing with peers.

- Performance of completed reading and writing activities.

- Content connections for reading and writing.

Recently educators have been talking about a balanced literacy program in which theory and learning strategies would be selected based on the learning styles of individual children. Such an approach reflects thoughtful maturity. Educators have reached a point where they feel comfortable saying, "It doesn't matter what the latest fad is, let's think about what's best for children." It appears that many teachers are comfortable being moderate or in the "radical middle."

Balanced instruction acknowledges the importance of skill development, but emphasizes both form (phonics, mechanics, etc.) and function (comprehension, purpose, meaning) and recognizes that learning occurs most effectively in a whole-part-whole context. The objective is to develop "engaged readers" (National Reading Research Center 1991)—strategic readers who possess multiple skills that enable them to read independently and comprehend what they read. Engaged readers use prior knowledge to gain new information from text read. They also have the ability to transfer and apply acquired information into new contexts. Engaged readers are motivated to read voluntarily, both for pleasure and for information (Morrow 1992). In addition, they often seek out others to gain new competencies (see Figure 1.1).

Motivation Theory and Literacy Development

Motivation is defined as an intrinsic desire to initiate, sustain, and direct one's activity.

FIGURE 1-1   Qualities of Engaged Readers

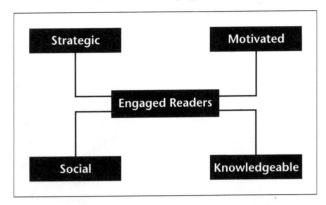

Motivated students return to and continue to work on tasks. Elements found to motivate children include:

- *The opportunity to have and make choices.* Choice gives children a sense of control and promotes motivation. Providing children with choices suggests that the classroom has a variety of literacy materials, spaces, and activities that students can decide to participate in.

- *Social collaboration.* Collaboration facilitates children's engagement in a task, but fostering collaboration requires time. The teacher needs time to guide literacy activities, and the children need time to practice literacy activities with peers, independent of the teacher. Collaboration can take many forms.

- *Challenging tasks.* Challenges promote goal attainment. Tasks must be challenging, but able to be accomplished.

- *Success.* Success gives students a sense of being competent. It is important for them to feel successful when completing tasks. Part of the success experience is sharing completed tasks with peers and teachers (Ford 1992; McCombs 1991).

When students have some control over their activities and feel challenged, competent, and successful in the performance of

these activities, they are more likely to participate (Spaulding 1992). Therefore, to establish classroom contexts that will enhance motivation, provide environments where students have choices of activities they are expected to participate in, where they feel that these activities are ones they believe they are competent to handle, and where, on completing the activity, they feel a sense of accomplishment and success. This combination helps to create motivated readers and writers.

The Value of Social and Physical Contexts for Learning

Social Contexts

When children work independent of the teacher, in collaboration with others, there is movement in the classroom, and more noise than when a teacher plays the traditional, dominant role of leading a lesson. Teachers wonder if learning can really take place in such an environment. They worry about how to get started, how to manage the situation, and how to help children learn to function independently in productive ways. A review of the literature on cooperative learning—that is, students working in small groups to help one another learn through discussion and debate—makes it clear that this type of learning context has many benefits. Researchers have found that interaction and collaboration among small groups of students promotes achievement and productivity (Johnson and Johnson 1987; Sharan and Sharan 1989–90). In addition, the interaction allows children to explain material to each other, listen to each other's explanations, and arrive at joint understandings (Johnson et al. 1981).

Cazden (1986) found that peer interaction allows students to try out many roles that they would otherwise be denied in the traditional student-teacher structure. In a cooperative learning setting more capable peers observe, guide, and correct while the student performs

During literacy center time Dharmesh and Imran read a newspaper article entitled "Cartoons Help Fight Drugs" and point out and discuss cartoon characters who are helping to solve the drug problem.

a task (Forman and Cazden 1985). Students are able to accomplish more together than they could alone. The peer interaction offers the same learning opportunities as tutoring.

According to Dewey (1966), children engaged in task-oriented dialogue with peers can reach higher levels of understanding than when teachers present information to them. Piaget (1959) suggests that peers serve as resources for one another in cognitive development. Also, in addition to fostering greater productivity and achievement, social settings seem to promote in students an intrinsic desire to learn because they become less dependent on the teacher (Wood 1990).

Physical Contexts

Preparing the physical environment of the classroom is often overlooked in planning. Teachers may concentrate on varying presentation strategies and interpersonal factors without considering the physical context in which teaching and learning occur. When program and environment are not coordinated, "setting deprivation" can result, a situation in which the physical environment fails to support teaching and learning activities (Spivak 1973).

Rather than serving only as a background for classroom activities, the physical environment has an important influence on teaching and learning. For example, rooms partitioned into smaller spaces improve verbal interaction and cooperation among students (Field 1980), and attractive literacy centers with a variety of materials increase use of such materials during free-choice periods (Morrow and Weinstein 1986). When teachers purposefully arrange space and materials in classrooms, the physical environment can motivate children to learn.

Children's Literature as Motivation

Children's literature is also an important source for motivating readers and writers.

Well-designed literacy centers provide an inviting area for children to read, write, collaborate on, and generally become involved with children's literature.

Arbuthnot and Sutherland (1977), Cullinan (1992), and Huck (1976) stress the importance of planned programs that encourage pleasurable experiences with literature. Such programs, they say, create interest in and enthusiasm for books. Teachers should read to children daily and discuss the stories they read and those their students read. Children should be encouraged to read to each other and to tell stories to the rest of the class. Books should be borrowed from school and taken home, and books from home should be brought to school and shared. Students' exposure to books and stories should be frequent and integrated with teaching in content areas. In addition to the motivational factors surrounding the use of children's literature, studies have revealed that students who use literature as a major part of their reading program tend to develop sophisticated language structures, enhance their vocabulary, and improve their reading comprehension and writing ability in both expository and narrative pieces (Cohen 1968; Morrow 1992).

Importance of Creating Independent Readers and Writers

Educators agree that reading is both a practical activity and a cherished and joyous privilege in life, yet not enough attention has been given to developing children's voluntary reading. Indeed, some of our methods for developing reading have discouraged children's interest in reading on their own. In a 1984 report to the U.S. Congress entitled *Books in Our Future*, Daniel Boorstin, Librarian of Congress at the time, warned that aliterates—individuals who can read, but choose not to do so—constitute a threat at least equal to that of illiterates in a democratic tradition built on books and reading. The practice or absence of independent reading, he wrote, "will determine the extent of self-improvement and enlightenment, the ability to share wisdom and the delights of our civilization, and our capacity for intelligent self-government" (p. iv). Aliteracy can be as devastating as illiteracy; as Mark Twain said, "Reading ain't no more use to him who don't read than him who can't."

Unfortunately, substantial numbers of children read neither for pleasure nor for information, although they have the cognitive capability to read (Applebee, Langer, and Mullis 1988). Some studies, which found that children do not spend a lot of time involved in voluntary reading, revealed a strong relationship between the amount of leisure reading one does and the degree of success in reading one achieves (Greaney 1980). In a study by Anderson, Fielding, and Wilson (1988), children recorded the number of minutes they spent reading outside of school. The researchers found a positive correlation between the number of minutes read and reading achievement. For example, children who scored at the 90th percentile on a reading test spent five times as many minutes per day reading books as children at the 50th percentile and more than two hundred times as many minutes per day reading books as children at the 10th percentile. In other studies, children's independent reading has been found to correlate positively with overall achievement in school (Cunningham and Stanovich 1991; Greaney 1980; Guthrie and Greaney 1991; Taylor, Frye, and Maruyama 1990).

Other studies have investigated the characteristics of home environments in which children have demonstrated voluntary interest in books or have established independent reading habits (Greaney and Hegarty 1987; Morrow 1983). These children were likely to be from small families, and their parents usually had educations beyond high school. The homes had rich literacy environments. Parents provided reading models for their children by reading often in their leisure time.

They read a variety of materials—novels, magazines, newspapers, and work-related documents. Books were placed in many different rooms, including the playroom, the kitchen, the bathroom, and children's bedrooms. Parents of voluntary readers took their children to the library often and read to them daily. They enforced rules regarding the television, regulating how much TV viewing could be done, and what types of programs could be watched. Voluntary readers were given a certain amount of independence and responsibility at home and participated in diverse leisure-time activities, not just reading, though their parents encouraged reading for their children as well as themselves. In short, these children were in settings where interactions between the adults and the children were socially and emotionally conducive to literacy growth (Clay 1976; Holdaway 1979; Moon and Wells 1979; Sakamoto and Makita 1973). We need to adapt the characteristics found in the homes of motivated readers to the classroom.

Voluntary readers also score well on reading tests at school (Hansen 1969; Lomax 1976; Morrow 1983). Anderson, Fielding, and Wilson (1988) found that children who were in classrooms that promoted independent reading did more reading at home than children from classrooms where there was little emphasis in this direction.

Despite these studies, too many educators still judge reading programs not by the personal reading habits of students but by scores on reading tests (Irving 1980; Spiegel 1981). According to the influential book *Becoming a Nation of Readers* (Anderson et al. 1985), learning to read requires having the motivation or desire, and practicing to achieve proficiency. In addition, to maintain fluency, reading should be a lifelong pursuit.

A recent survey of educators, most of whom were classroom teachers, indicated that creating a motivation for or an interest in reading is of major importance in teaching children to read. Those surveyed, a random sample of International Reading Association members, felt that more research was needed in the area of motivating readers (O'Flahavan et al. 1992). Since children's reading habits develop early in life (Bloom 1964), schools must deliberately attract children to reading during the early years, or voluntary reading may never become a lifelong habit.

Format of This Book

In this book I hope to provide practical ideas on motivating children to become independent readers and writers. These ideas are based on research that was carried out over several years and that involved children, teachers, and parents. The students ranged from preschool through sixth grade, and from high to low socioeconomic status (SES); they came from diverse cultural and racial backgrounds (Morrow 1982; 1983; 1992; Morrow, O'Connor, and Smith 1990; Morrow and Weinstein, 1982; 1986). The research was designed to discover elements in classrooms that promoted children's interest in reading and writing and to demonstrate the ability to create motivated students who chose to read and write independent of adults both in and out of school.

I focus on the social and physical contexts that foster independent reading and writing. These include:

1. Physical layouts that encourage literacy instruction in the classroom, in particular the design of literacy centers.

2. Teacher modeling literature activities that provide guidance, develop children's skills, and encourage independent use of materials and strategies.

3. Specific time for collaboration during independent reading and writing.

These things give children a feeling of competence about their literacy ability and put them in control of decisions about literacy tasks they would participate in.

These contexts thus foster the processes of socially interactive literacy activity during periods of independent reading and writing. These processes in turn result in the following outcomes:

1. Enhanced appreciation for reading and writing.

2. Improved reading comprehension, language, and writing development.

3. Voluntary participation in cooperative reading and writing by all children, including those with special needs.

4. Changed teacher behavior and beliefs.

In the many classrooms in which I have worked, teachers and children gave different names for independent reading and writing periods: recreational reading period, rec reading time, voluntary reading period, independent reading and writing period, reading and writing workshop, writing and reading appreciation program (WRAP), and literacy center time, the two favorites being the last two. For that reason, in this book I will refer to cooperative periods for independent reading and writing as either WRAP time or literacy center time.

CHAPTER 2

Designing a Literacy Center: "It's Cozy and Makes You Want to Read"

The comments that follow were made by third graders who participated in cooperative activities with their peers in their classroom's literacy centers (Morrow 1992):

- "The literacy center is the best part of the classroom! You get to read with your friends and they help you and you help them."

- "I like using the literacy center because you can choose the books you want to read. You can choose fat books, skinny books, story books or information books. It's cozy there; you can lean on the pillows or sit in the rocking chair to read."

- "There are so many fun things in the literacy center that it makes you want to read and write. My favorites are the felt stories, tape stories, and roll movies."

- "You get to read a lot when you have your own classroom library because the books are right there. I'm reading so much and practicing so much, which will help me get better at it."

- "The only thing the literacy center needs to make it better is a snack bar where you can get some food, so you can eat and read."

The following are comments by teachers who created literacy centers in their classroom:

- "Children who would never read are reading in the literacy center. They enjoy the choice of all the materials there."

- "I think the carpet is a magic carpet; I'm going to call it the reading rug. Kids who never read before will sit on that little piece of rug and read."

- "My children have a sense of pride about the literacy center. They helped to create it and contribute their reading and writing materials to it. It is indeed a special spot in

"The literacy center is the best part of the classroom! You get to read with your friends and they help you and you help them."

our classroom—a splash of color, a ray of light, and a place for happiness."

But what does such a classroom look like? What does the teacher do to motivate students to pursue literacy activities in a social setting? The following describes a classroom in the process of developing a dramatic play center that would integrate play, literacy activities, and the content area theme.

With each thematic unit, Mrs. Millson helps her children design the dramatic play center to reflect the topic being studied and to enhance the opportunity for meaningful experiences with reading and writing. When learning about animals, the students in her combination first and second grade decided to create a veterinarian's office. The class had the opportunity to visit a veterinarian to help with their planning. They began redesigning the dramatic play area by creating a waiting room with chairs and a table filled with magazines and books. Mrs. Millson suggested hanging posters and pamphlets about good health practices for pets, which she had obtained from the veterinarian. The children made a poster that listed the doctor's hours, and added signs that said "*No Smoking*" and "*Check In with the Nurse When You Arrive.*" The nurse's table contained forms for patients to fill out, a telephone, telephone books, appointment cards, and a calendar. The veterinarian's office also contained patient folders, prescription pads, white coats, masks, gloves, cotton swabs, a doctor's kit, and stuffed animals. Blank paper, a stapler, pencils, markers, colored pencils, and crayons were placed in the area as well. The classroom computer was taken from the math center and relocated into this area for keeping patient records and other files. The center design was a collaborative effort by the teacher and children.

After preparing the environment with the children, Mrs. Millson modeled the use of various materials. She suggested to them, "While you're waiting for your turn to see the doctor, you can read to your pet in the waiting area

In the thematic play area designed as a veterinarian's office Josh, who acted as the doctor, examined Tim's teddy bear and said, "This teddy bear needs to stay in bed, keep warm, and get lots of rest until his cold is gone." Then he wrote the prescription: "10 PLS EVRY HOUR."

and the nurse can ask you to fill out forms. The receptionist might like to talk to patients on the phone about problems their pets are having, schedule appointments, and write out appointment cards. You can write bills for visits, accept payments, and give receipts. The doctor can fill out prescription forms and write up patient reports." Later, Mrs. Millson joined the children in the dramatic play area, pretending to be the nurse, then the doctor, so that she could model the types of literacy behavior for children to try.

A week later, the children were fully engaged in this center. Jonnell sat in the waiting room reading the story *Caps for Sale* to her pet monkey. Damien joined her with his pet rabbit and listened. He took a turn reading. Katie, who was taking the role of the nurse, called Jonnell to answer some questions about her monkey's problems. When Jonnell finished filling out forms, she watched Damien's pet while he spoke with the nurse. Josh was acting as the doctor, examining a stuffed teddy bear that was brought in by Tim. Josh wrote the animal's name and the owner's name on a file folder, and then picked up the prescription pad. He told Tim, "You see this?

Now this says to make sure that your teddy bear takes 10 pills every hour, until he feels better. This teddy bear needs to stay in bed, keep warm, and get lots of rest until his cold is gone." Then he wrote "10 PLS EVRY HOUR" on the pad.

Let's look more closely at what's going on here. The teacher, along with the children, prepared the physical environment. She described and modeled the use of materials in the literacy-enriched role playing area; after this initial guidance, she helped students in need of direction. As the children became more involved, the teacher allowed the play to take place on its own, and she participated in the children's activities. The social collaborative setting provided opportunities for purposeful communication. The dramatic play theme allowed for the integration of play, literacy, and content. During their role playing, children pursued real-life behavior that involved meaningful and functional literacy activities. The teacher in this classroom was aware that a classroom environment that encourages children to communicate in varied ways helps motivate them to read and write (Morrow 1990).

Positive Effects Related to Planned Physical Environments

Students' behavior and interactions are influenced by the classroom environment, and classroom design is a critical factor in the success of instruction (Loughlin and Martin 1987). Historically, physical environment has played an important role in fostering learning. Montessori, for example, featured a "prepared environment" as the central part of her educational program (Morrison 1988). She prepared special materials for learning and carefully designed appropriate child-sized furniture where manipulatives were easily accessible and visible. Montessori planned the placement of items in the classroom to be sure optimum learning could take place in a self-directed, independent manner.

Research has shown many ways in which the physical design of the classroom affects the children's behavior. Rooms partitioned into smaller spaces help to increase verbal interaction and cooperative activities among children more than rooms with large open spaces (Field 1980). Children in carefully arranged rooms show more creativity and productivity and greater use of language-related activities than children in randomly arranged rooms (Moore 1986; Nash 1981). Literacy-enriched dramatic play areas based on themes stimulate literacy activities and the enhancement of literacy skills (Morrow 1990; Morrow and Rand 1991; Neuman and Roskos 1990, 1992). Dramatic play with story props improves story production and comprehension, including recall of details and ability to sequence and interpret (Mandler and Johnson 1977; Saltz and Johnson 1974). Enhancing the physical setting of literacy centers increases children's use of this area, which results in their doing more reading and writing, thus improving their literacy achievement (Morrow 1992).

The physical environment also influences teachers' behavior. When instruction takes place in quality spaces, teachers are more sensitive and friendly toward children. They are more apt to teach students to consider the rights and feelings of others and encourage them to choose activities. Teachers in poorer-quality environments are less involved and less interested, are more likely to teach arbitrary social rules, and are more restrictive (Kritchevsky and Prescott 1977).

Given these findings, a classroom designed to promote optimum literacy development will offer an abundant supply of materials for reading, writing, and speaking. While the majority of these materials are concentrated in the literacy center, literacy materials are also provided in content area learning centers.

Materials and settings throughout the classroom simulate real-life experiences and make literacy meaningful for children. They are based on information children already possess, and are functional so that children can see a need and purpose for using literacy.

Physical Environments That Motivate Reading and Writing

Instead of viewing the physical environment as background or scenery for teaching and learning, teachers can purposefully arrange the space and materials, thus acknowledging and using the physical environment as an active, positive, and pervasive influence on instruction (Loughlin and Martin 1987; Morrow 1990; Rivlin and Weinstein 1984; Sutfin 1980).

Classroom Layout and Materials

A literacy-rich classroom usually contains centers dedicated to particular activities or content areas appropriate to the grade level, such as social studies, science, math, art, music, dramatic play, block play, and language arts. Each centers contains materials pertinent to the content area in general and materials specific to topics currently under study. Resources are primarily devoted to the content area, but are designed to develop literacy skills as well. The materials are manipulative and activity oriented, and designed so children can use them either independently or in small groups. Figure 2.1 shows a typical floor plan for preschool through first-grade classrooms, and Figure 2.2 shows one for second- through fifth-grade rooms. Because of space limitations and the fact that older children may change classrooms for different subjects, it is sometimes more difficult to have multiple centers beyond the early childhood grades. However,

a literacy center can be used to house materials that might ordinarily be found in other centers. A box or shelf can also serve as a center. "Centers" can simply be places to house materials; actual work can be done in other parts of the classroom.

The following are suggestions of various kinds of classroom centers, with materials that could furnish each center. Of course, teachers should adapt these suggestions to suit their own needs and preferences and those of their children.

- *Science center.* The science center could include such items as an aquarium, a terrarium, plants, a magnifying glass, a class pet, magnets, a thermometer, a compass, a prism, shells, rock collections, a stethoscope, a kaleidoscope, a microscope, informational books and children's literature that reflect topics being studied, and blank journals for recording observations of experiments and scientific projects.

- *Social studies center.* The social studies center could contain maps, a globe, flags from other countries, posted materials on current events, artifacts from other countries, informational books and children's literature that reflect topics being studied, writing materials to make class books, and personal books about themes being focused on.

- *Art area.* The art area could contain watercolor paints, brushes, colored pencils, crayons, felt-tip markers, various kinds of paper, scissors, paste, pipe cleaners, scrap materials (bits of fabric, wool, string, etc.), clay, play dough, food and detergent boxes for sculptures, books about famous artists, posters of artists' work, and directions for making crafts.

- *Music area.* The music area could house a piano, a tape recorder with varied musical tapes, rhythm instruments, songbooks, songs that have been made into books,

FIGURE 2-1 Classroom Floor Plan for Preschool Through First Grade

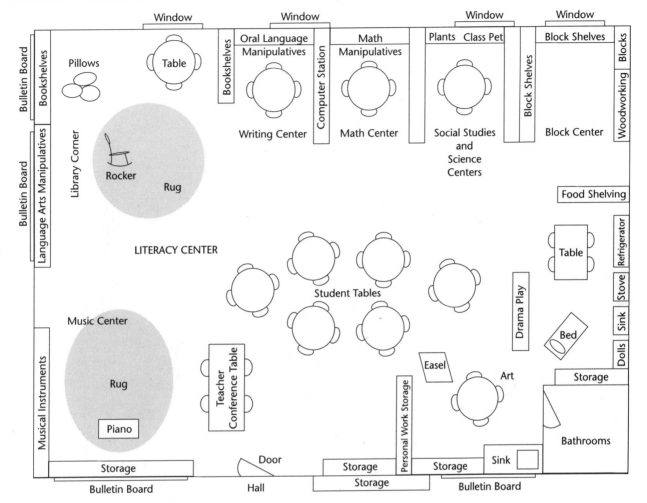

books about famous composers and singers, sheet music, and charts containing song lyrics.

- *Mathematics area.* The math area could contain scales, rulers, measuring cups, movable clocks, a stopwatch, a calendar, play money, a cash register, a calculator, dominoes, an abacus, a number line, a height chart, an hourglass, numbers (felt, wood, and magnetic), fraction puzzles, geometric shapes, math workbooks, children's literature about numbers and mathematics, writing materials for creating stories, and books related to math.

- *Block area.* The block area would contain, of course, blocks of different sizes and shapes,

but it could also contain figures of people and animals, toy cars and trucks, items related to themes being studied, paper and pencils to prepare signs and notes, and reading materials related to themes.

- *Dramatic play area.* Items promoting dramatic play include a telephone, food cartons, plates, silverware, newspapers, magazines, books, a telephone book, a cookbook, note pads, cameras and a photo album, and a table and chairs. The dramatic play area can be transformed into settings for theme-related role playing, such as a grocery store, a pet shop, a gas station, or a restaurant. Materials for reading and writing related to the theme should also be available.

FIGURE 2-2 Classroom Floor Plan for Second Through Fifth Grade

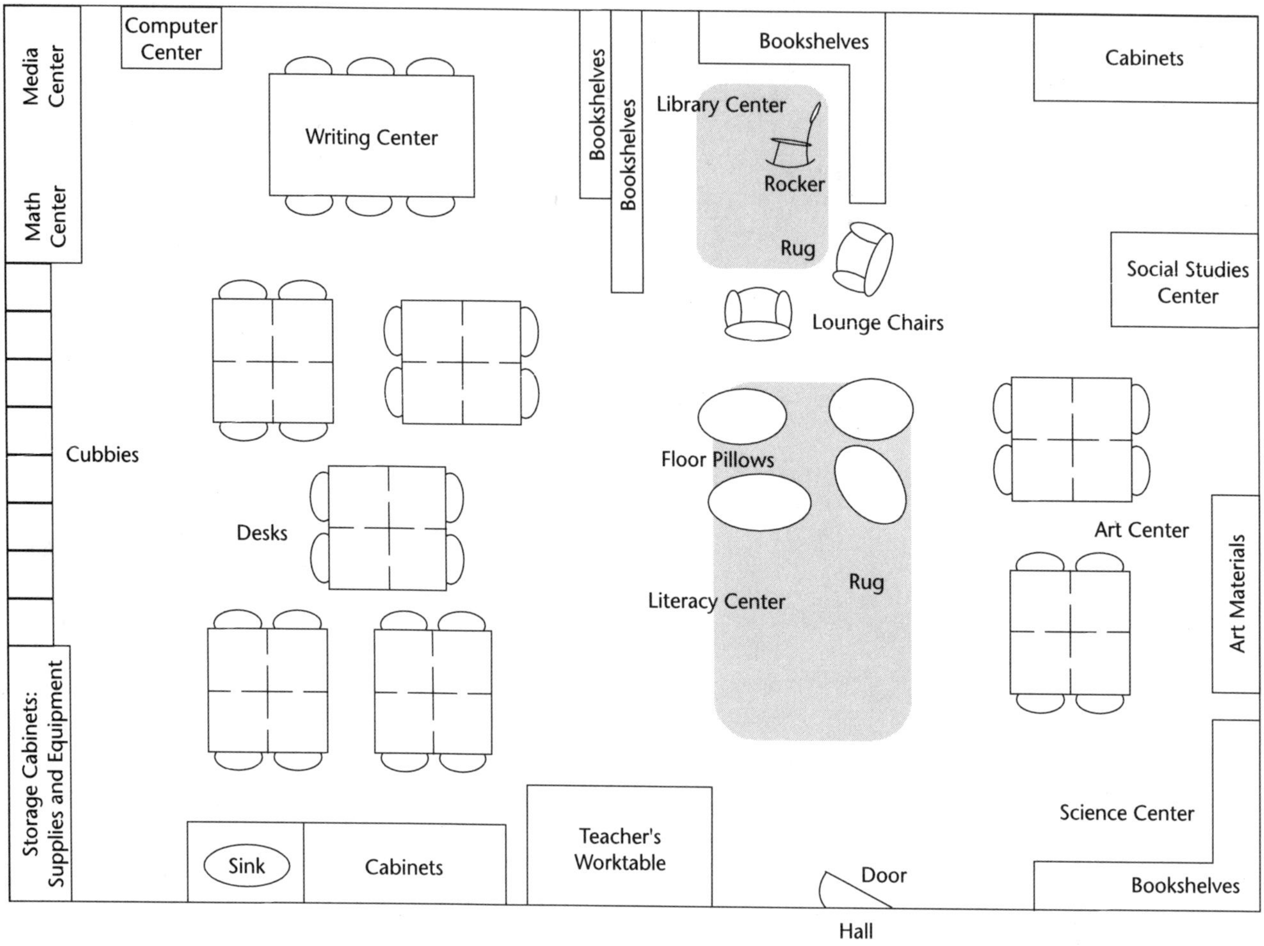

Furniture that is part of a center can also serve as partitions to separate centers. Center materials may be stored on tables or shelves, in boxes, and on bulletin boards. These materials, as well as the center itself, should be accessible and labeled. Each piece of equipment in a center should have its own designated spot so that the teacher can direct children to specific items and children can find and return them easily. Typically, at the beginning of the school year, most centers hold only a few items; new materials are added as the year progresses. Before new items are placed in centers, the teacher introduces their purpose, use, and placement (Montessori 1965).

The room design should support whole-group, small-group, and individual instruction. The teacher can hold large-group lessons when the children are sitting at their desks or tables, or sitting on the floor. The literacy center and the music center are usually large enough for the entire class to meet together. A teacher conference table can provide space for small-group or individualized instruction. This table can be used for skill development that is guided by the teacher. The conference table should be placed in a quiet area of the room to facilitate the kind of instruction that occurs around it, but it should also be situated so as to allow the teacher to see the rest of the room where children are working independently. The various centers offer settings for independent and self-directed learning. In general, as can be seen from the classroom floor plans in Figures 2.1 and 2.2, centers are positioned so that areas where quiet work is typical (the literacy, math, social studies, and science centers) are away from the more noisy, active centers (dramatic play, blocks, art).

Having enough space for centers is always a problem. In small rooms, centers are often just storage areas for materials that are used outside of the area. For example, materials may be in boxes, on a bulletin board display, or on a door to a closet. During center time, furniture in the classroom can be moved to provide for working space. Also, as mentioned earlier, not all classrooms will have all centers mentioned, especially in the upper grades. Teachers may need to collaborate and share centers by creating different centers in different rooms, which students can use when they change rooms for different subjects.

such as "Quiet Please" and "Please Put Materials Away After Using Them." Charts labeled "Helpers," "Daily Routines," "Attendance," and "Calendar" can simplify classroom management (Morrow 1997; Schickedanz 1993). A notice board placed prominently in the room can be used to communicate with children in writing and for children to communicate with the teacher and other children. Experience charts display new words generated from themes, recipes, and science experiments. This environmental print needs to be used with the children, or it may go unnoticed. Children should be encouraged to read and copy it, and to use words from the labels in their writing.

Functional Environmental Print

Literacy-rich classrooms are filled with visually prominent functional print, such as labels on classroom items and areas. Signs communicate functional information and directions,

Creating the Literacy Center

Much of what we know about the contexts of early literacy development emerged from research on the home environment of chil-

Literacy-rich classrooms are filled with visually prominent functional print, such as labels on classroom items and areas. Signs communicate functional information and directions.

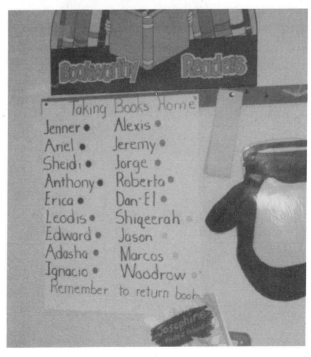

dren who read early without direct instruction (Durkin 1966; Strickland and Taylor 1989; Teale 1978, 1986). Even though the home setting cannot be replicated in school, the classroom environment can be adapted to reflect the physical and social contexts that affect home literacy experiences. For example, one feature of a rich home literacy environment that can be easily incorporated in classrooms is to have a large variety of literacy materials: novels, magazines, newspapers, work-related papers, picture books, blank paper, pads, crayons, and other writing instruments. In fact, the overall goal of creating a literacy center is to provide a homelike environment in which reading and writing occur frequently and naturally in a social setting.

To convey the importance of literacy and books as a principal source of knowledge, the classroom library should be the focal area of the room (Stauffer 1970). Although a central school library is vitally important, classroom libraries provide several benefits. For one thing, they offer immediate access to literacy materials (Beckman 1972). In addition, they prompt children to read more. Bissett (1970) found that children in classrooms with library collections read 50 percent more books than children in classrooms without such collections. An increased use of literature also occurred during free-choice periods in classrooms that had well-designed library corners (Anderson, Fielding, and Wilson 1988; Ingham 1981; Morrow 1982, 1983; Morrow and Weinstein 1982, 1986).

Design

When I began working with teachers, it became apparent that the standard classroom design would not promote the types of social, cooperative, and independent behavior we wanted to encourage. To meet this goal and keep literacy experiences meaningful and functional, we needed an area for the display, storage, and use of literacy materials—the literacy center. Not only would the literacy center hold a variety of literacy-related materials and be a place for children to collaborate when using them; it would also be a symbolic, functional, and motivating factor for fostering literacy behavior.

In the course of many research projects, I spoke with teachers about changing the physical design of their classrooms to incorporate a literacy center. Their immediate concern was having enough space. Some of the comments I heard were: "It will be too much trouble to change everything." "It will be upsetting to the children." "I just can't fit it into my room!" It was already difficult fitting in the instructional materials they had, along with the children's desks and the children. How would it be possible to fit one more item in their classroom?

We discussed rearranging desks and other pieces of equipment to find ways to fit literacy centers in their classrooms. Some teachers were skeptical at first, but they began to see the possibilities as we went from one classroom to the next discussing where the center might be placed and how it might be created. I shared photographs I had illustrating what other classrooms looked like before and after literacy centers were added, and we visited rooms similar to theirs that had centers created in them.

In some classrooms we were able to design the entire literacy center in one section of the room. In others, we had to separate sections. For example, in older buildings with few electrical outlets, the headsets and tape players that needed electricity were often placed away from the rest of the center.

The size of the room affected the type of literacy center. In very small rooms the center also had to be small. Instead of being a work space, it became a place to house the materials that children took to use in other parts of the room. In some larger classrooms teachers extended the literacy center so that it was not confined to one section but spilled out into other areas of the room.

Various formats were tried in different classrooms to find the elements that were effective for each room and each teacher. Teachers began to think of the classroom as a second home for both their students and themselves and decorated it with the same care as their home. Like interior decorators, they would discuss placement of furniture, purchase needed items, and coordinate color. Bright colors were often chosen for pillows, rugs, bulletin board coverings, and posters. In what were often very drab-looking environments, we wanted the centers to make a statement about the importance of literacy.

Children were consulted about the design of the centers. Together, the teacher and the children decided where the center would be placed, what materials should be included, and what types of books should be acquired. When the children in one class were asked what kind of books they'd like to have in the center, Roseangela immediately replied, "We need a lot of science stuff, that's all Marcel likes to read." Chris said, "I want motorcycle magazines and ones about trains." Mercedes had a special interest in Africa and wanted some informational books and storybooks on that topic. This triggered the children's interest in books about other countries; they eventually added books about Italy, Japan, Mexico, Israel, and Ireland.

The teacher's preferences were a major factor in the way the centers were arranged. Teachers wanted to discuss plans with me, their colleagues, and their students. For example, Ms. Peters collaborated with me concerning the design of her center, but she wanted to put the area together herself. She used most of the materials I suggested, but she also implemented her own ideas, such as a system for checking out books.

The completed literacy centers were attractive and functional additions to classrooms that were often in poor physical condition. After using them for a time, the teachers commented on their success (Morrow 1997):

- "I never thought that I would have enough space in my classroom for a literacy center. I was surprised that so many materials could fit into such a small area."

- "The literacy center became a place where children of all reading and writing abilities mingled. . . . This social context seemed to provide an atmosphere for cooperative learning. The children looked forward to their time there each day."

- "The children were a great help in deciding what to put where and in setting up the area. Because they were a part of designing the literacy center, they were particularly proud of that area."

- "Children participated in the literacy center quite naturally and with enthusiasm. Children read more, wrote more, and took more books home from school than any other group of youngsters I had in my classroom before. I think it's because the materials were so attractive and accessible. It suddenly dawned on me that while children had the opportunity to use the centers, they were practicing skills I'd been teaching them during direct instruction."

By the end of the school year, the teachers and children had made some changes to all their centers to accommodate their individual needs. I was delighted with the changes, since it showed that teachers were taking an interest in the area and responsibility for it. In most cases, teachers added more pillows, stuffed animals, literature manipulatives, new books, and other ideas that we hadn't thought of to make the area unique for them and their students. We were pleased with how well the centers were cared for and how much they were used. Figure 2.3 shows a typical literacy center.

Furnishings

The literacy centers were a focal point of their classrooms, a spot that was immediately

FIGURE 2-3   A Literacy Center

visible and inviting to the children or anyone who walked into the room. Bookshelves, cabinets, partitions, or freestanding bulletin boards were used to provide a sense of privacy and physical definition to the area. The size of the literacy center varied with the size of the classroom, but generally it could accommodate five or six children comfortably. Equipment was chosen to attract children to the literacy center and provide a comfortable area to read, write, and collaborate.

An area rug measuring from 4 by 6 feet to 5 by 8 feet allowed children to work on the floor. Pillows, beanbag chairs, and stuffed animals added an element of softness.

A table and some chairs in the literacy center provided a spot for reading, writing, and listening to taped stories.

In school, children rarely have any privacy. To meet this need for children to be by themselves to read and think, we created a "private spot." A large, decorated appliance box often became the private spot, but children found spaces on their own under tables and other such areas in the classroom where they could be alone to read and think.

We used adult-sized rocking chairs in all the centers. These chairs were an immediate hit. The rocker became a special place, which we named "The Literacy Chair of Honor," since the teacher sat here to read stories to the children and guest storybook readers used the rocker as well. Children cuddled together in the chair to read during literacy center time. The rocking chair provided the opportunity for the children to take the role of the teacher and read their original stories to each other, perform puppet stories they had created, or tell about wonderful books they had read. The homelike quality of the rocking chair, along with the rug, pillows, and stuffed animals, set a tone during story reading that reflected

FIGURE 2-4 Bulletin Board for Leaving and Receiving Messages

Holdaway's (1979) Shared Book Experience, in which story reading is modeled on the best features of the home bedtime story experience.

To make the area as inviting as possible, attractive posters that encourage children to read were obtained from the American Library Association (50 East Huron Street, Chicago, IL 60611). Teachers prepared bulletin boards to promote reading as well. One popular bulletin board featured a hot air balloon that held two children in its basket with the saying "Get Carried Away: Read and Write" (Figure 2.4). Other bulletin boards featured favorite authors.

At the end of the school year, when children were asked what they liked about the periods of independent reading and writing, materials in the literacy centers were frequently included in their comments. Tara said she especially liked the pillows and teddy bears. Her friend Lauren added, "I like the animals you get to hug when you read." Jason said that what he liked best was "lying down on the carpet and reading a book with my head on the pillows." Teshan said, "I like to sit on the rug in the Book Nook and read, but the rocking chair is the best of all!"

The Book Collection

Two kinds of bookshelves were incorporated into the literacy center. The major collection of books was kept on shelves with their spines facing out. Usually shelves already in the classroom were used. Plastic crates turned on their side were added as needed for extra space. To call attention to featured books about themes being studied, open-faced bookshelves were used; these allowed the covers of the books to be seen. Open-faced bookshelves included the floor-standing wooden type, or those that sat on a shelf, made of wood or corrugated cardboard. We also used wire racks that swivel and stand on the floor, and teacher-made shelves of corrugated cardboard.

About twenty-five new books were rotated on and off the regular bookshelves about once a month to stimulate interest. Books on the open-faced shelving were changed with new themes that were studied, holidays celebrated, and so forth. All the books were shelved by category and color-coded according to the type of book. For example, the poetry books were marked with a blue dot and placed on a shelf marked "Poetry." Setting up an organizational system provided a good opportunity to make connections between the school library and the classroom library.

Children were encouraged to check books out to take home. Loose-leaf binders were used for record keeping, with each child's name on a different page. Using different colored binders helps the child identify where his or her checkout page is, and also helps avoid having to wait in line for the book. Some teachers used a sign-out sheet on clipboards. Others used two file boxes, one for books checked out and one for books returned. Cards were filled out and placed in the "out" box when they were checked out of the classroom and put in the "in" box when they were returned.

The resource section provides sample forms for book checkout (pp. 99–101).

Five to eight books per child were typically included in the literacy center book collection. These spanned three or four grade levels and appealed to a variety of interests. When we found that many children enjoyed reading what a friend was reading, we stocked multiple copies of favorite books. Magazines and current newspapers were also included. To meet all the children's needs and interests, we found it essential to include the following varied selection:

- *Picture concept books* are designed for young children. Each book focuses on a theme through the use of pictures. Examples of picture concept books include *Let's Eat* (Fujikawa 1975) and *Wheels* (Byron 1981).

- *Picture storybooks* are the most familiar type of children's literature. In these books, text and illustrations are closely associated. Picture storybooks such as *Owl Moon* (Yolen 1987) and *Where the Wild Things Are* (Sendak 1963) are ideal for reading aloud. These books cover a wide range of topics, and the best are fine literature.

- *Easy-to-read books* have large print and limited vocabulary. They are designed to help beginning readers succeed on their own. Stories include repetition and rhyme to make the text predictable. Books by Dr. Seuss, such as *The Cat in the Hat* (1957) and *Green Eggs and Ham* (1960), fit into this category.

- *Traditional literature* includes fables, folktales, nursery rhymes, and fairy tales. Many of these stories originated in other cultures and thus can broaden a child's experience and knowledge base. Stories in this category include *Why Mosquitos Buzz in People's Ears* (Aardema 1975) and *Saint George and the Dragon* (Hodges 1984).

- *Informational books* are nonfiction and usually relate to a content area such as science or social studies. Some books, such as the *Magic School Bus* series (Cole 1987, 1990), mix fiction with fact.

- *Newspapers and magazines* should be included as literacy center selections. Many are created especially for children. For example, *Ranger Rick*, a magazine with a science focus, is published by the National Wildlife Federation. Another popular magazine is *Highlights for Children*, which includes stories, jokes, riddles, crafts, information about all content areas studied in school, and material for many grade levels. Newspapers help to make connections from the classroom to real life.

- *Biographies* to include in the book collection would be those of individuals that would be of interest to children—sports figures, past presidents, television celebrities, or inventors.

- *Big Books* are usually large versions of smaller picture storybooks. They can also be original stories. These oversized books rest on an easel in order to be read. The purpose of Big Books is for children to be able to see the print as it is being read, to make the association between oral and written language, and to notice how the print is read from left to right across the page.

- *Novels* are longer books about one topic that are divided into chapters. They are considered for children from second grade on up.

In addition to these categories, other sorts of books can be useful and popular: joke and riddle books, cookbooks, craft books, books made from songs, participation books (which allow children to touch, smell, or manipulate features), books related to television shows, and books in a series built around familiar characters.

One can never tell which children will be attracted to which books. That is why having a varied collection is so important. Yassin, for example, a robust boy who was retained in second grade, attended basic skills classes to help improve his low reading achievement. He often read from cookbooks, which we would never would have expected. One day he asked his teacher, "Ms. Peters, you got flour at home?" When Ms. Peters said yes, Yassin asked, "You got eggs?" Ms. Peters nodded. "How about chocolate and nuts?" asked Yassin. "I have that, too," answered Ms. Peters. "That's good," said Yassin. "If you bring that into school we can all bake brownies, 'cause that's the stuff you need. I read it in this book." Yassin came from a home with no parents. His elderly grandmother, who was sick a great deal,

took care of him. He read the cookbook to get closer to his vision of home-cooked food.

Manipulatives

Literacy manipulatives increase children's involvement in the center. Manipulatives such as puppets, felt boards with characters from children's literature, and taped stories with headsets motivate children to engage in storytelling, storybook reading, writing (Morrow and Weinstein 1986), and, eventually, sustained silent reading, an activity that does not include manipulatives. We found that at first the manipulatives were a major attraction, but as time went on, more book reading occurred and the manipulatives were used less. However, they remained a source of ideas for children to create and present their own reading and writing projects.

All the manipulatives that pertained to a specific story were accompanied by the relevant book. Children added to the supply as they made their own manipulatives and came up with new ideas. Materials were stored in clear, zip-lock plastic bags, which were easily identified and kept in a special spot set aside for them. Following are brief descriptions of what the manipulatives are and how to create them. Chapters 3 and 4 discuss the use of these materials.

Felt Board Story   For a felt board story, characters are created out of felt or construction paper. The figures are then laminated or covered with clear contact paper to protect them, then backed with felt or sandpaper so that they can stick to a felt board as the story is told. The felt board can be purchased or made by gluing felt onto a wooden board, a cork board, or cardboard. A felt board should tilt backwards to help the figures stay on.

The resource section provides specific instructions on how to make a story board (pp. 130–131).

Roll Movie   The roll movie manipulative is a box made to look like a television. A hole is cut in the box, and in the box is a series of pictures on rolled paper. Dowels are inserted through the top and bottom of the box, and the paper is attached to the dowels and rolled either from top to bottom or from left to right. The dowels are turned to change the scene. Stories may be drawn on computer paper, taped-together 8 1/2-by-11-inch sheets, or white shelving paper sold in rolls at the supermarket.

The resource section provides specific instructions for making a roll movie box (p. 164).

The box is covered with colored contact paper to withstand classroom use. Teachers who model the use of the roll movie should not be too concerned about artistic quality. In fact, if the teacher's roll story is too professional-looking, it could intimidate the children and make them feel that their illustrations aren't good enough. Not every scene from a story needs to be illustrated; it is best to select those that are crucial for the sense of the story.

Headsets and Taped Story   Tape-recordings of various pieces of children's literature can provide a model for good reading. Tapes are kept in plastic bags with the original book so the children can follow along as they listen. Commercially produced tapes of books are available from companies such as Scholastic, but it is easy enough for teachers and students to create their own. Teachers, parents, and children can all record tapes.

Prop Story   Prop stories involve the collection of appropriate materials for a particular book. The props are then used when reading or telling the story. For example, when telling *Strega Nona* (de Paola 1975), a story in which a magic pasta pot bubbles out of control, the teacher can bring in a large pot and pretend to stir pasta with a big spoon while telling the story.

Puppet Story   Various types of puppets may be used for storytelling, including hand puppets, stick puppets, face puppets, and finger puppets. The resource section provides diagrams for making puppets (see pages 135–145).

Chalk Talk   Chalk talks are presentations of stories that are drawn as they are told or read. Pictures may be drawn on a chalkboard or on large sheets of easel paper. The main character in a story may be made from oaktag and slipped onto the storyteller's hand with an elastic band that is attached to the figure, to make it appear as if the character is drawing the story.

The resource section provides some sample chalk talk stories (pp. 147–154).

The Author's Spot

Because reading and writing are linked (Pappas, Kiefer, and Levstik 1990), each literacy center should include an area for writing. This can be called "the author's spot." Materials in the author's spot should provide children with the opportunity to experiment with writing and later to edit and publish their work (Bissex 1980). Children will base their writing on their experiences with environmental print and texts, on their perception of others' modeling, and on own interactions with peers and adults.

The author's spot may include a table and chairs, and many writing materials, such as colored markers, crayons, pencils (both regular and colored), chalk, and a chalkboard. Various types of paper may be available, including unlined white paper or newsprint, and sizes as large as 24 by 36 inches may be used. Index cards allow children to record their "Very Own Words." The word collections can be stored in file boxes, decorated coffee cans, or plastic baggies (one per child). A writing folder for each child holds writing samples over the course of the school year. A computer is another important piece of equipment for writing in the literacy center.

Materials for making books are essential, including paper, a hole punch, a stapler, and construction paper for covers. Blank books prepared by the teacher or children, especially ones keyed to special occasions, such as books in the shape of a leaf in the fall or a flower in the spring, invite children to fill in written messages and stories. Children's literature in the classroom collection is a catalyst for writing.

See the resource section for some specific ideas (pp. 209–212).

A bulletin board for children to display their own selected pieces of writing can be useful. Equally valuable are message or notice boards used to exchange messages among members of the class and the teacher. Teachers can use the message board to send messages to individual children as well as to post important information for the class as a whole. Mailboxes, stationery, envelopes, and stamps for youngsters' incoming and outgoing mail may be placed in the writing center if a pen-pal program is under way.

One day I was rushing to a school when I realized I didn't have the booklets I'd planned to provide for the writing center. I grabbed instead some university blue books used for taking exams. This turned out to be serendipitous. The books have 12 to 16 pages, come in packs of 50, and are inexpensive. I called the booklets "author's books," and the children used them to write special stories and as journals. Teachers ordered more when the original supply ran out.

Publishing books is a favorite activity, and the materials for binding books (plain white paper, needle and thread, cardboard, contact paper, and glue) are easily accessible. Older children can make their own; younger children may need help, perhaps by parent volunteers in the classroom. Children's original books, complete with a title page citing author and illustrator, are catalogued and

The resource section provides specific directions for making children's books and Big Books (pp. 209–212).

made part of the classroom library. These original books are often checked out by other children and may become popular choices for reading material. Teachers and children can also make Big Books as class projects.

Manipulatives for Learning Word Analysis Skills

In this volume the emphasis is on reading and writing through the use of literature. Therefore all of the materials discussed in depth deal with using children's literature to develop skills. There are, however, other important approaches to literacy development that focus on word analysis skills, such as phonics, the use of context and syntactic clues, picture clues, configuration, sight words, syllabication, punctuation, spelling, and structural analysis. Many materials are available to help students develop these skills. These materials come in the form of magnetic boards with letters, activity books, puzzles, and games, including those based on television game shows such as *Jeopardy, Wheel of Fortune,* and *Concentration* and other popular games such as "Spill and Spell" and "Scrabble." Such games allow children to learn and practice prefixes, suffixes, consonant sounds, digraphs, and vowel sounds, among other things. Materials that develop word analysis skills also belong in the literacy center, to be used by students during periods of independent and collaborative work.

Acquiring Materials

One of the concerns many teachers I worked with had about creating a literacy center was how to acquire the needed materials. A literacy center can be outfitted at low cost with a little creativity. The most important step is to acquire enough books for a classroom library. Donations from homes can be requested, and a box put in the school hallway for collecting books. One school suggested that children donate a book to their classroom on their birthday instead of bringing in favors for their classmates. Many children's book clubs, such as Scholastic, Troll, and Weekly Reader, award bonus points based on the amount of books purchased by the children in a class. These bonus points can be exchanged for free classroom books. Inexpensive books can also be found at flea markets and garage sales. In addition, school and town libraries should not be overlooked. Books can be rotated regularly from the school's collection to supplement the classroom library.

Parents should be involved in school programs and share responsibility for gathering materials for the children's learning environment. Parent-teacher organizations can be asked for help in fund-raising or creating manipulatives. In one school, where I had designed literacy centers in all the second-grade classrooms, parents voiced their concern that children in all grades should have the advantage of such an environment. After discussion, a plan was made to have a research assistant coordinate a parent workshop to make materials for all the classrooms. Parents met in the school library for five sessions, once each week, during which time they created felt stories, roll movies, props, and other manipulatives to use with children's literature. They made enough materials to outfit forty classrooms! A group of parents in another elementary school set up a publishing center. Once a week parent volunteers would come in to bind books that the children had written for publication. All the materials were donated by parents and local businesses.

In districts where it is difficult to get the help of parents I have had the art teacher work with me. She in turn enlisted the help of children in sixth grade through high school, who made many of the materials needed to create complete literacy centers for the elementary school classrooms. They delivered the materials they created and modeled them for the children. This made the endeavor a truly cooperative one.

A Literacy Center Checklist

Figure 2.5 is a checklist for teachers who are designing literacy centers for their classrooms. The checklist asks teachers to look in other parts of their classroom for materials that create rich literacy environments. The

FIGURE 2-6   Centers and Theme Materials

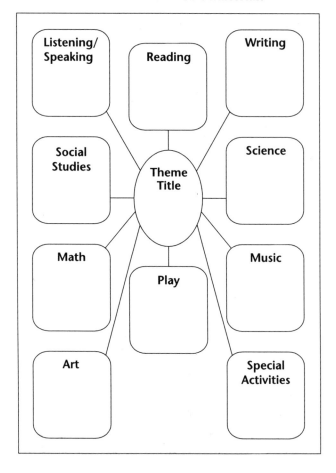

FIGURE 2-5 Checklist for Evaluating the Classroom Literacy Environment

	Yes	No
The Literacy Center		
1. Children participate in designing the center (develop rules, select a name for center, develop materials, etc.).	_____	_____
2. Area placed in a quiet section of the room.	_____	_____
3. Visually and physically accessible, yet partitioned off from the rest of the room.	_____	_____
4. Rug, throw pillows, rocking chair, beanbag chair, stuffed animals.	_____	_____
5. Private spot in the corner such as a box to crawl into and read.	_____	_____
6. Uses about 10 percent of the classroom space and can fit five or six children.	_____	_____
The Library Corner		
1. Bookshelves for storing books with spines facing outward.	_____	_____
2. Organizational system for shelving books.	_____	_____
3. Open-faced bookshelves for featured books.	_____	_____
4. Five to eight books per child.	_____	_____
5. Books represent three or four grade levels of the following types: picture books, picture storybooks, traditional literature, poetry, realistic literature, informational books, biographies, chapter books, easy-to-read books, riddle and joke books, participation books, series books, textless books, TV-related books, brochures, magazines, newspapers.	_____	_____
6. Twenty-five new books circulated every four weeks.	_____	_____
7. Check-out/check-in system for children to take books out daily.	_____	_____
8. Headsets and taped stories.	_____	_____
9. Felt board and story characters with related books.	_____	_____
10. Materials for constructing felt stories.	_____	_____
11. Other story manipulatives (roll movie, puppets, etc., with related books).	_____	_____
12. System for recording books read.	_____	_____
13. Multiple copies of the same book.	_____	_____
The Writing Center (Author's Spot)		
1. Tables and charts.	_____	_____
2. Writing posters and bulletin board for children to display their writing.	_____	_____
3. Writing utensils (pens, pencils, crayons, felt-tip pens, colored pencils, etc.).	_____	_____
4. Writing materials (many varieties of paper in all sizes, blank booklets, pads).	_____	_____
5. Typewriter and/or computer.	_____	_____
6. Materials for writing stories and making them into books.	_____	_____
7. A message board for children and teacher to post messages.	_____	_____
8. A place to store Very Own Words.	_____	_____
9. Folders in which children can place samples of their writing.	_____	_____
10. A place for children to send private messages to each other.	_____	_____
11. Manipulative materials for developing word analysis skills.	_____	_____
The Rest of the Classroom		
1. Environmental print, such as signs related to themes studied, directions, rules, functional messages.	_____	_____
2. A calendar.	_____	_____
3. A current events board.	_____	_____
4. Appropriate books, magazines, and newspapers.	_____	_____
5. Writing utensils.	_____	_____
6. Varied types of paper.	_____	_____
7. A place for children to display their literacy work.	_____	_____
8. A place for teachers and children to leave messages for each other.	_____	_____
9. Print representative of multicultural groups present in the classroom.	_____	_____
10. Content area centers present in the classroom (besides the literacy center) (circle those appropriate):		

music   art   science   social studies   math   dramatic play checklist suggests content area centers and describes basic materials to include in these centers. When studying specific themes such as animals or plants, teachers should add literacy materials and other items to the literacy center and content area centers. Figure 2.6 provides a map for teachers to use while studying new themes during the year. The map is used for listing new books and other materials to be added to the literacy center and content area centers. Teachers I have worked with have taken the ideas presented in this chapter and improved on them, adapting them to their own style and needs.

Modeling Literature Activities: Motivating Reading and Writing

When it was story time in Mrs. Monroe's first grade the children quickly put aside what they were working on and hurried over to the literacy center. The children moved around until they were all in comfortable positions on the rug. Mrs. Monroe sat in the rocking chair, where she always read aloud. She showed the children the caterpillar they had found on the playground, which was now in their terrarium. The class was studying insects, focusing on what they eat and how they grow. After talking about how the caterpillar moves and eats, Mrs. Monroe took out the book *The Very Hungry Caterpillar* (Carle 1970) and said, "I'm going to tell a story today about a caterpillar who is very hungry. Listen for all the things that he eats in this story and see how many you can remember. Also what you think is factual information about caterpillars in this story and what you think is fiction." As she talked, she put on a green caterpillar sock puppet that extended from her hand halfway up her arm. In the story the caterpillar eats many things, such as a strawberry, an apple, and a piece of cherry pie. Next to the teacher were cutouts for the food mentioned in the story, with a hole cut in the middle of each. Every child was given a cutout so they could participate in the story reading. As a food was mentioned, the child with the cutout of that food put it onto the teacher's arm as if feeding the caterpillar. After the story, the class discussed what the caterpillar had eaten and what they thought was factual information in the story and what was fiction. Then Mrs. Monroe put the book and story props in the literacy center and reminded the children that they could work together and retell this story during literacy center time.

The caterpillar puppet with its story props was an instant favorite. Warren put on the puppet and Michael read the story while referring back to the book. A few other children joined in by offering the caterpillar some food cutouts. While Mary waited for a turn with the puppet, she asked Tamika if she wanted to write a story about a caterpillar who didn't want to be a butterfly. The two girls gathered some paper and markers and settled down under a table to write. First they drew some pictures and then they added captions. Kevin, Erin, and Kim began work on a felt story of *The Very Hungry Caterpillar,* which they presented to the class during story time later that week.

Mrs. Kimmel, a fifth-grade teacher, had just finished reading the short novel *Sadako and the Thousand Paper Cranes* (Coerr 1977) to her class. The novel is about a twelve-year-old Japanese girl who develops leukemia as a result of radiation from the atomic bomb that was dropped on the city of Hiroshima in Japan. In the book, Chizuko visited her friend Sadako in the hospital. She had a gold-colored square piece of paper. "Watch!" she said, and she folded the paper over and over, turning it into a beautiful crane. "If a sick person folds one thousand paper cranes," Chizuko said, "the gods will grant her wish and make her well again." Sadako folded 644 cranes before she died at the age of twelve. Her classmates folded the rest. Mrs. Kimmel's objective was to introduce the children to Japanese culture through their literature and the art of Japanese paper folding, called origami. She also wanted to discuss the consequences of war, an issue that connected with what the class was studying in social studies. Mrs.

See the resource section for directions on folding an origami paper crane (p. 182).

Kimmel guided the discussion of the differences between this novel and stories about children in America. The second part of the discussion revolved around the consequences of war. To help them further understand the culture, at the end of the discussion Mrs. Kimmel gave each student a sheet of instructions with a diagram for making an origami paper crane. Children worked in pairs to help each other.

After these guided lessons, during literacy center time, Mrs. Kimmel's and Mrs. Monroe's children worked collaboratively using stories, props, and activities the teachers had mod-

Children involved in center work.

eled. The children were self-directed and independent. Their motivation came from the teacher-guided literature activities done in class. These teachers created a climate in their classrooms where reading and writing were pleasurable, exciting, and meaningful activities. The children wanted to read and write because they had discovered the joy of literature, the satisfaction in learning information, and the pleasure in sharing ideas. How did these first-grade and fifth-grade teachers encourage this to happen?

From a theoretical perspective, Mrs. Monroe and Mrs. Kimmel provided support and guidance that enabled children to participate in activities they could not have done on their own (Vygotsky 1978). Gradually, through practice, the children became self-directed, claiming responsibility for their own learning. The demonstration of materials and guidance in their use made these items more interesting to the children. The children were also given the opportunity to work in social settings to explore and practice.

Using Children's Literature

Using literature with children is an important way to motivate them to become readers

and writers. Pleasurable experiences with literature create an interest in and enthusiasm for books. In addition, studies reveal that children who use literature as a major component in their reading instructional programs tend to develop sophisticated language structures, enhanced vocabulary, and improved reading comprehension and writing ability in both expository and narrative pieces (Cullinan 1992; Huck 1976; Morrow 1992).

Teachers should read every day to children in the elementary grades and discuss the stories read. Children should be encouraged to read to each other and discuss the books among themselves. Books can be borrowed from school and taken home, and books from home can be brought to school and shared with others. Exposure to books and stories should be frequent and integrated with teaching in the content areas.

Teacher-guided literature activities model pleasurable literature activities for children, motivate children's enthusiasm for and voluntary use of literature, and prepare children for self-directed, collaborative literature activities in literacy centers. A whole-class activity modeled by the teacher might have the teacher in a rocking chair reading a story with the children sitting on the rug. In a small-group activity the teacher and students might all be on the rug or at a table provided for small-group work.

When I began to work with teachers on activities to motivate reading and writing, they were concerned about the time it would take to add such activities to all that they already needed to accomplish in their literacy programs and content area subjects. We discussed the fact that the activities I was suggesting would also develop skills and teach content; and if children could be motivated to participate in reading and writing voluntarily in and out of school, this would enable them to practice and improve skills taught. Together we decided that the teachers would try to carry out three to five guided pleasurable literature activities each week. To many it seemed impossible; however, the teachers found many opportunities to include literature. They could use literature to teach skills, and they could present literature in content area subjects. The literature activities being suggested were to mesh or blend with more traditional literacy activities.

In the following sections are strategies that teachers found were most enjoyable for students to participate in. They motivated children to read and write voluntarily, enhanced literacy development, and encouraged social learning (Morrow, O'Connor, and Smith 1990; Morrow 1992, 1997). Activities were carried out in the literacy centers, since the centers provided the appropriate setting and climate for such lessons.

Reading Aloud

As explained earlier, the importance of reading to children regularly and using literature in the school curriculum is well known (Anderson, Fielding, and Wilson 1988; Cullinan 1987; Stewig and Sebesta 1978). Exposure to children's literature helps children enhance literacy skills, including vocabulary and syntactic development, phonemic awareness, decoding skills, and the ability to comprehend text (Feitleson, Kita, and Goldstein 1986; Hoffman, Roser, and Farest 1988). Reading aloud to children is a daily event that teachers and children find rewarding. It provides an opportunity for children to experience literature pleasurably, discuss ideas about books read, and relate books to content area instruction.

To make the story readings as pleasurable as possible, teachers should read in a relaxed atmosphere and in the same location every day. If there is a rocking chair in the classroom, this is the perfect place for the teacher to sit. Children can sit on a rug on the floor or in chairs, but they should be close to the teacher, who should be in a position to be seen by all. The teacher should always read the material in advance in order to be familiar with the text. If there are illustrations in the book they should be shown during the reading. Expressive readings, in which different voices are used for different characters, is a good reading strategy. Children also enjoy facial expression and animation on the part of the reader. This helps the book come alive. Different genres should be used, and books selected that are appropriate for the children in the classroom. Selections should be tied to the children's interests, personal experiences, and topics being studied. Books that the children themselves may not be able to read, such as sophisticated novels, read a chapter at a time, are good choices, as are books with beautiful illustrations and interesting language. Young children enjoy rhyme, repetitive phrases, and conversation. In addition, stories read to children should have a clear plot structure that includes the following elements:

- *Setting:* Descriptions of time, place, and characters.

- *Theme:* A problem or goal faced by the main character.

- *Episodes:* A series of events that helps the main character achieve his or her goal or solve his or her problem.

Teachers and special visitors read aloud to students.

- *Resolution:* The main character accomplishes the goal or solves the problem, and there is a clear ending to the story.

Directed Listening or Reading

The directed listening (or reading) thinking activity (DLTA or DRTA) is a general strategy teachers can use to guide story readings. When used it should be modeled—presented in a way that prompts students to use it themselves. There are three parts to this strategy:

1. A pre-story discussion that provides background knowledge and sets a purpose for listening or reading.

2. The reading of the text, with comments and questions.

3. A post-story discussion that relates to the purpose for listening.

The DLTA or DRTA can focus on any of a number of things—comprehension development, a content area theme, illustrations, even just the fun of reading. Having a purpose to direct the children's reading or listening is the key for getting them involved with

the literature presented. The two examples at the beginning of this chapter showed the method at work. Children should be reminded to use the strategy when they read something new.

Questions That Engage Students

Conversation about the book can vary, but it can begin with the teacher's asking some questions about the book. *Efferent* questions usually deal with expository material and the details in a passage. Questions that deal with *aesthetic* issues provoke responses that can be personalized to children's experiences, feelings, and interests, and so are more likely to motivate engagement. The following questions have been found to spark lively discussion:

- Was anything especially interesting to you in the story? Funny? Sad? Scary? Exciting?

- If you could change part of the story, what would it be?

- If the story continued, what do you think would happen?

- Has anything similar to what occurred in the story ever happened to you?

- Does the story remind you of another story or TV show?

- Have you known people like the characters in the story?

- Pretend you are a character in the story. What does it feel like?

- What was your favorite part of the story?

- Was there a part of the story you didn't like?

In the following excerpt second graders were asked if the story they had just read, *The Legend of the Bluebonnet: An Old Tale of Texas* (de Paola 1983) reminded them of another

Small groups of children interact with the teacher and each other.

story they knew about. This was the rich response that occurred:

Alison: It reminded me of another book.

Teacher: What book was that?

Alison: *The Legend of the Indian Paintbrush.*

Suzanne: Me, too, because it kind of relates. *The Legend of the Bluebonnet* that we read is a folktale and so is *The Legend of the Indian Paintbrush* and Tomie de Paola did both of those books—retold and illustrated—and She-Who-Is-Alone in *Bluebonnet* wanted something green very badly and Little Gopher in *The Legend of the Indian Paintbrush* wanted something very badly too. So they have lots of things alike.

Text-related or efferent responses are also important, to be sure students are comprehending the main ideas of the story. Efferent discussions are especially appropriate for expository texts in content area subjects. Asking children to retell a story in sequence and to discuss details can be valuable.

Small-Group and One-to-One Story Readings

Small-group and even one-to-one reading are also useful in fostering interest and com-

prehension. These formats allow children to respond more than they can in whole-group reading. The children create the meaning of the story through their participation (Holdaway 1979). For example, during conference time one day, Mrs. Johnson read portions of *The Mountains of Tibet* (Gerstein 1987) to Davida, Ryan, and Alison. She asked what they found especially interesting. The kind of in-depth conversation that followed (Johnson 1995, p. 60) would be difficult in a whole-group setting.

Davida: It was interesting and puzzling when the galaxies talked to him.

Mrs. Johnson: What do you think was going on then?

Davida: I don't really know. It was puzzling when the animals talked. Well, but animals make their own noises, but they don't talk.

Mrs. Johnson: Um, let's go back to that galaxy and voice part. There was a voice that talked from the galaxies. What do you think that was about?

Ryan: I think it was God.

Alison: I think it was God, too.

Mrs. Johnson: How about you, Davida? You said you were puzzled by it.

Davida: I don't know, really.

(*Davida was silent while the other children took turns; then she reentered the conversation.*)

Davida: I thought since it was a book, they [the galaxies] could be speaking to him [the main character].

Alison: Yeah, authors can do what they want.

Repeated Readings

Reading a book more than once can be a pleasurable experience, like singing a favorite song. As a result of repeated readings, children develop favorite books that they ask for over and over. One class asked for *Strega Nona* (de Paola 1975) so often that the teacher asked me for reassurance that repeating the story could still be a valuable learning experience. The fact is, repeated readings allow children to be more interpretive in their understanding. Their familiarity with the story allows them to predict outcomes, make associations, and form judgments (Morrow 1988; Yaden 1985). Also, as a result of repeated readings of books children become familiar with story structure models.

The following is taken from a transcription of a kindergarten child's response to a third reading of *The Little Red Hen* (Galdone 1975b). For the sake of brevity, this excerpt includes only the child's comments and questions and the teacher's responses; most of the story reading has been omitted.

Teacher: Today I'm going to read the story *The Little Red Hen*. It is about a hen who wanted some help when she baked some bread. (*The teacher begins to read the story.*) . . . "Who will help me to cut this wheat?" (*she reads*).

Melony: "Not I," said the cat. "Not I," said the dog. "Not I," said the mouse.

Teacher: That was good, Melony. You are reading. (*The teacher continues to read, but Melony stops her.*)

Melony: I want to read that part, but I don't know how.

Teacher: Go ahead and try. I bet you can, I'll help you. It starts: "The cat smelled it."

Melony (chiming in): "The cat smelled it, and she said, 'Umm, that smells good.' And the mouse smelled it, and it smelled good . . . "

(*After finishing the story the teacher asked Melony if she wanted to say anything else about the story.*)

Melony: I want to find the part where it says that the animals were so bad that they couldn't have any cake. (*Melony searches through the book.*) There it is, almost at the end. She's going to make a cake and she'll say "Who's going to bake this cake for me?" And the cat says, "Not I," the dog says, "Not I," the mouse says, "not I." And then when she's cooking it they smell a good thing and then they wanted some, too, but they didn't have any, 'cause they didn't help with the work.

Teacher: You're so right. They didn't help do the work, so they didn't get to eat the cake.

Melony: Where does it say "Not I"? Show me the words in the book.

Teacher: Here it is. See if you can find it on this page.

Melony: I found it. Oh look, there's the word dog, dog, dog. (Morrow 1997, p. 210)

This example demonstrates the value of repeated reading in both comprehension and print awareness, and it appears to be a very pleasant experience for children.

Favorite Authors and Illustrators

Authors and illustrators of favorite books should be discussed and highlighted. For example, Mrs. Meyers read the story *A Letter to Amy* (Keats 1968) and the class discussed the illustrations. Jason said, "Those pictures look like real people, but they look like they're painted, not like photographs." Mrs. Meyers pointed out how Keats uses a collage of painting, newspaper, wallpaper scraps, and other materials to illustrate his books.

Children can write letters to their favorite authors and illustrators. Eventually they will begin to think of themselves as authors and illustrators. In one classroom, Melissa was writing an original story entitled "The Man Called Why." After writing the title on the cover of the book she added "Story and Illustrations by Melissa," showing her own self-confidence as an author.

When possible, teachers should arrange for authors and illustrators to visit the class. The Children's Book Council has published a pamphlet on how to arrange for authors to visit. Send $2.00 and a self-addressed, stamped envelope to: Artist Visits, Children's Book Council, 568 Broadway, Suite 404, New York, NY 10012.

Additional Reading-Aloud Activities

There are many more strategies to increase children's enjoyment of literature and to provide good models. Mrs. Colon invited guests each week to come to her third-grade ESL classroom and read to her students. Readers included the school principal, the custodian, parents, high school athletes, children from older grades, and a school bus driver, as well as the superintendent, the town mayor, and an author. Not only did this show that people from diverse backgrounds valued reading, it also provided a sense of excitement and novelty to hear many different people read. Mrs. Colon took photos of all of the individuals who read to her class during the year and created an exciting bulletin board with the pictures.

Children should be encouraged to bring books from home to share with the class and to take books home to share with their family.

Books published by the children themselves may be chosen as read-aloud books. These may prove especially popular and can encourage the children to write their own stories for publication.

When books featuring food are read, the class can prepare the food. Blueberry muffins were baked in Mrs. Gables's first grade after she read *Blueberries for Sal* (McCloskey 1948). Mrs. Youseff's class made fruit salad after reading *Mister Rabbit and the Lovely Present* (Zolotow 1962), jam sandwiches after reading *Bread and Jam for Frances* (Hoban 1964), and vegetable soup after reading *Stone Soup* (Brown 1947). In fourth grade, Mrs. Tofel's class made chocolate after reading *The Chocolate Touch* (Catling 1979).

> The resource section provides the titles of more books featuring food that can be prepared in the classroom (pp. 171–174).

Television and film can be powerful tools in drawing children to books. Many fine pieces of children's literature have been adapted for television or movies, from *The Cat in the Hat* (Seuss 1957) for young children, to *James and the Giant Peach* (Dahl 1988) for older children. Be aware of books that are featured on TV and encourage children to watch such programs. Then use the books for classroom discussion.

Storytelling and Retelling

Storytelling is a very effective strategy to get children excited about literature. It establishes rapport between the listener and the teller because of the eye contact that occurs. Long pieces of literature can be shortened to accommodate attention spans. Teachers should first model storytelling and then encourage children to participate in the activity. Storytelling is an art, but it can be mastered by all.

Many of the teachers I worked with had not used storytelling as a specific technique before. We discussed how it was done and reviewed suggestions that would improve their chances of success. We also told stories to each other to gain confidence. The following points were found to be essential in effective storytelling:

- Know the story well but don't memorize it.

- Use catch phrases or important words from the story.

- Be expressive.

- Look directly at the audience.

- The length of the storytelling depends upon the attention span of the audience.

- Encourage audience participation when possible.

- Practice the story before telling it.

- Always have the book available to connect with the printed word.

Story retelling by children offers active participation in a literacy experience and helps youngsters develop language structures, comprehension, and a sense of story structure. Retelling a story, whether orally or in writing, enhances comprehension and organization of thought. It also allows for personalization of thinking, as children mesh their own life experiences into their retelling. Retelling is a holistic strategy, in contrast with the more traditional piecemeal approach of teacher-posed questions that require the recall of only bits of information. Also, as they gain experience in retelling children assimilate the concept of story structure. They learn to introduce a story with its setting. They recount its theme, plot episodes, and resolution. In retelling stories, children demonstrate their comprehension of story details and sequence. They also infer and interpret the sounds and expressions of characters' voices. Retelling is not easy for children, but with practice they improve quickly. To help children develop the practice of retelling, it is best to let them know before they read or listen to a story that they will be asked to retell it. Props such as felt board characters or pictures in the text can be used to help students retell the story. Teachers need to model retellings or storytelling. The following procedure is helpful in guiding a child's oral retelling (with written retelling, teachers may prefer to have the child write the entire story first and then confer with him or her using the following guidelines).

First, ask the child to retell the story. "A little while ago, I read the story [Name the story]. Would you retell the story as if telling it to a friend who has never heard it before?" If needed, the following prompts may be used:

- If the child has difficulty beginning the retelling, suggest beginning with "Once upon a time" or "Once there was . . ."

- If the child stops retelling before the end of the story, encourage him or her to continue by asking, "What comes next?" or "Then what happened?"

- If the child stops retelling and cannot continue even with the general prompts above, ask a question that is relevant at the point in the story at which the child has paused—for example, "What was Jenny's problem in the story?"

If a child is unable to retell the story, or if the retelling lacks sequence and detail, the retelling may need to be prompted, step by step, with one or more of the following (Morrow 1997, p. 212):

- "Once upon a time" or "Once there was . . ."

- "Who was the story about?"

- "When did the story happen?" (Day, night, summer, winter?)

- "Where did the story happen?"

- "What was [the main character's] problem in the story?"

- "How did [he or she] try to solve the problem? What did [he or she] do first [second, next]?"

- "How was the problem solved?"

- "How did the story end?"

Retelling can be used to develop many types of comprehension. The prompts, of course, should match the goals.

Following is an example of the interactive behavior that can take place between a teacher and kindergarten child in a first story retelling.

Teacher: Philip, can you tell me the title of the story I just read to you today?

Philip: I don't know.

Teacher: Let's look at the cover of the book and see if that helps you remember. It was about a turtle. Can you remember his name?

Philip: Oh yeah. *Franklin in the Dark* [Bourgeois 1986].

Teacher: That was very good, Philip. You remembered the whole title of the story without my help. Now can you retell the story as if you were going to tell it to your good friend Patrick. Now Patrick hasn't ever heard this story so you don't want to leave anything out when you tell it to him. Why don't you try and start to tell the story.

Philip: Okay. *Franklin in the Dark*. One time Franklin didn't want to go in his shell. He was too scared. But his mama said, "There's nothin'" in there." But Franklin didn't want to go in the shell because there was monsters in there. He didn't like to go in because he was afraid. At the end he went in 'cause his mama got him a night light in his shell. So he turned on a light night light and went to sleep. And that's it.

Teacher: You did a fine job, Philip. You remembered Franklin's problem, or the theme

of the story, and how Franklin and his mother solved the problem at the end of the story. Let's look at the book and see if there is anything else you could include in your retelling. (*The teacher and Philip start to look through the book.*)

Philip: Oh yeah, I forgot stuff. Franklin went for a walk and he saw lots of animals who were scared of things. There was a lion who was afraid of loud noise, so he put on earmuffs.

Teacher: Were there any other animals?

Philip: Yeah, well . . . there was this bird who was scared to fly high so he got a great big balloon thing to help him fly.

Teacher: The thing he used was called a parachute. Did he meet anyone else?

Philip: I don't know, I'm tired.

Teacher: Okay, I'll help you out. There was a polar bear who was afraid of the cold so he wore a snowsuit to keep him warm; and there was a duck who was afraid of deep water, so he used water wings when he went swimming.

Philip: Oh yeah, that's right.

Teacher: Philip, you did really well today. When you have some time, why don't you take the book and look at the pictures and try to tell the story again.

Suitable Books

Story retelling is not an easy task for young children. Books selected should have clear plot structures that make their story lines easy to follow and therefore easy to retell. Other elements, such as repetitive phrases, familiar sequences (use of days of the week, numbers, letters, etc.), conversation, and general familiarity or popularity of the plot or characters, can add to a story's predictability and thus aid retelling. Following is a short list of predictable books suitable for retelling:

- *Books with repetitive phrases*:
  Are You My Mother? (Eastman 1960).
  Brown Bear, Brown Bear, What Do You See?
  (Martin 1967).
  It Looked Like Spilt Milk (Shaw 1947).

- *Books with familiar sequences*:
  The Very Hungry Caterpillar (Carle 1970).
  Ten Bears in My Bed (Mack 1974).
  Chicken Soup with Rice: A Book of Months
  (Sendak 1962).

- *Books with conversation*:
  The Gingerbread Man (Arno 1970).
  Ask Mr. Bear (Flack 1971).
  Mister Rabbit and the Lovely Present (Zolotow 1962).

- *Popular and familiar stories*:
  Goldilocks and the Three Bears (Galdone 1972).
  The Little Red Hen (Galdone 1975b).
  Caps for Sale (Slobodkina 1974).

- *Stories with good plot structures*:
  Peter's Chair (Keats 1967).
  Swimmy (Lionni 1963).
  The Tale of Peter Rabbit (Potter 1902).

When children retell together with the use of props, such as a felt board with story figures, often one does the telling and the other manipulates the materials. They will sometimes then switch roles. One child begins, then the other takes over, taking turns throughout a given retelling. As two or more children retell together, they can offer assistance to one another as needed, such as offering prompts about what comes next or correcting mistakes in the retelling.

Following is a retelling by two first graders using a flannel board. Patrick retells the story, while Charlene puts the characters on the board. Charlene offers prompts and corrections, and fills in parts Patrick leaves out.

Patrick: There was these three billy goats, a big one, a little one and, um . . .

Charlene: It's the medium one you forgot.

Patrick: The goats had no grass on their side of the water, so the little one goes over the bridge to get some grass. The troll says, "I'm going to eat you up."

Charlene: No, the troll says, "Who's that trip-trappin' over my bridge?" And the little goat says, "It is me, the little one," and then the troll says, "I'm goin' to eat you up."

Patrick: The little one says, "I'm too little, my middle brother's comin'," and the troll said, "Then be off with you." The middle goat comes and the troll say, "Who's that trip-trappin' on my bridge?" "It is me, the middle one." "I'm goin' to eat you up." The middle one says, "I'm too small, here comes my big brother." Charlene, put up the big goat.

Charlene: Okay, I'm gonna tell some now. The big goat came, and the troll said, "Who's that trip-trappin' over my bridge?" "It is me, the big goat," said the big one. "Come on, come over," said the troll.

Patrick: I'm finishing. Now he knocks him in the water.

Charlene: No, not yet. The troll says, "I'm gonna knock your eyeballs into your ears."

Patrick: And that's what the goat done. He knocks the troll in the water. That's the end.

Charlene: No it's not, Patrick. You have to say, "And the billy goats lived happily ever after," and now it's the end.

When children retell novels they cannot retell the entire story as they do for picture storybooks. To retell a novel, children should be asked to summarize the main idea of the book, or to retell the part they liked best or the chapter they enjoyed most.

Using Retelling and Rewriting as an Assessment Tool

Story retellings and asking children to rewrite stories can be used to measure a child's

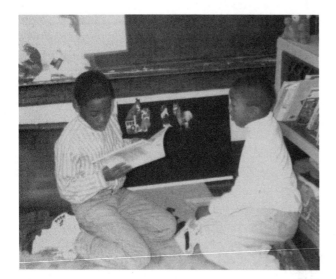 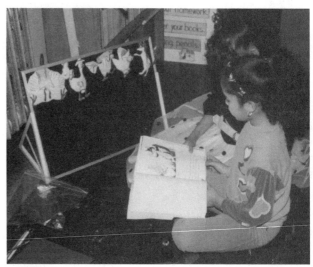

Children retell stories using the felt board with story characters.

comprehension of a story (Morrow 1992). Through analysis of a retelling or rewriting, one can diagnose a child's ability for literal recall (remembering facts, details, cause and effect relationships, and sequencing of events). Retellings can reveal a child's sense of story structure. For example, does a child's retelling include statements of setting, theme, plot episodes, and resolution? Through retelling, children also reveal their ability to make inferences as they organize, integrate, and classify information that is implied but not expressed in the story. They may generalize, interpret feelings, or relate ideas to their own experiences (Irwin and Mitchell 1983; McConaughy 1980). Because holistic comprehension is revealed through a child's retelling, this method of assessing comprehension seems to have an advantage over the more traditional, piecemeal methods of asking specific questions (Morrow and Weinstein 1986).

A child's story retellings and rewriting can be assessed several times during a school year to evaluate change. When a child's retelling is to be evaluated, the child should be informed of that fact before the story to be retold is read. During the retelling for evaluation, the teacher should not offer prompts. He or she may, however, encourage children to offer their best by saying when they pause, "Can you think of

anything else about the story?" or "You are doing very well. Can you try to continue?"

To assess a child's oral or written retelling for its sense of story structure or inclusion of structural elements, the teacher should first parse, or divide, the events of the story into four categories: setting, theme, plot episodes, and resolution. The teacher then notes the number of ideas and events that the child accurately includes within each of the four structural categories, regardless of their order. A story guide sheet, outlining the parsed text, is used to help tabulate the ideas and events the child includes in the retelling. The child receives credit for a partial recall or for recounting the gist of a story event (Pellegrini and Galda 1982; Thorndyke 1977). Having checked off the child's inclusion of elements, the teacher observes sequence by comparing the order of events in the child's retelling with the actual story. The analysis indicates not only which elements a child includes or omits and how well a child sequences, but also where instruction might be necessary to develop an area where the child's retelling has been particularly weak. A comparison of retellings over a year will illustrate if the child has progressed.

The following outline presents the events or parsed story for *Jenny Learns a Lesson*

(Fujikawa 1980), a story about a little girl who likes to play pretend games and invites her friends to do so. When her friends come to play, Jenny tells everyone what to do. After several such episodes, her friends leave, angry because of Jenny's bossing, and do not return. Jenny is lonesome and realizes her problem. She apologizes to her friends, invites them back to play, and promises not to boss them. They agree to play and this time all pretend as they wish. The parsed story is followed here with the transcription of a seven-year-old child's oral retelling of the story, then an analysis of the retelling. This same type of analysis can be used with a written retelling of a story (see Figure 3.1).

Parsed Story: *Jenny Learns a Lesson*

Setting

Once upon a time there was a girl who liked to play pretend.

Characters: Jenny (main character), Nicholas, Sam, Mei Su, Shags the dog.

Theme

Every time Jenny played with her friends, she bossed them and insisted that they do what she wanted them to.

Plot Episodes

First episode: Jenny decided to pretend to be a queen. She called her friends to come and play. Jenny was bossy and told them what to do. The friends become angry and leave.

Second episode: Jenny decided to play dancer, with the same results as in the first episode. (She calls her friends to play. She tells them what to do. The friends leave.)

Third episode: Jenny decided to play pirate, again with the same results.

Fourth episode: Jenny decided to play she was a duchess, again with the same results.

Fifth episode: Jenny's friends decided not to play with her again because she was so bossy. Many days passed and Jenny became sorry for being bossy.

FIGURE 3-1 Quantitative Story Retelling Analysis for Sense of Story Structure

Child's Name___Beth_____ Age ____7_____
Name of Story _Jenny Learns a Lesson_ Date _____

Directions: Give 1 point for obvious recall and "gist." Give 1 point for each character named as well as words such as *boy* and *girl*. Credit plurals (*friends*) with 2 points.

Setting
a. Begins story with an introduction.   1
b. Names main character.   1
c. Number of other characters named.   2
d. Actual number of other characters.   4
e. Score for "other characters" (c/d).   .5
f. Includes statement about time or
   place.   1

Theme
Refers to main character's primary goal
   or problem to be solved.   1

Plot Episodes
a. Number of episodes recalled.   4
b. Number of episodes in story.   5
c. Score for "plot episodes" (a/b).   .8

Resolution
a. Names problem solution/goal
   attainment.   1
b. Ends story.   1

Sequence
Retells story in structural order: setting,
   theme, plot episodes, resolution.
   (Score 2 for proper, 1 for partial,
   0 for no sequence evident.)   1

Highest score possible: 10   Child's score: 8.3

* Use checks instead of numbers to determine elements included and progress over time. Retellings can be evaluated for interpretive and critical comments (Morrow 1997).

Resolution

The friends all play together and each person did what he or she wanted to do.

They all had a wonderful day and were so tired that they fell asleep.

Sample Verbatim Transcription, Beth, age 7

Once upon a time there's a girl named Jenny and she called her friends over and they played queen and went to the palace.

They had to, they had to do what she said and they didn't like it, so then they went home and said that was boring . . . It's not fun playing queen and doing what she says you have to. So they didn't play with her for seven days and she had . . . she had a idea that she was being selfish, so she went to find her friends and said, I'm sorry I was so mean. And said, let's play pirate, and they played pirate and they went onto the pretend boat. Then they played that she was a fancy lady playing house. And then they have some tea. And they played what they wanted and they were happy . . . The End.

Children should play an integral part in evaluating their oral and written retellings. As a teacher evaluates a child's retelling a child can do the same with his or her own form. The following is an assessment discussion about an oral retelling (Morrow 1997, p. 217).

Teacher: Beth, let's read the transcription of your retelling together. (*They both began to read. The teacher lets Beth read alone as long as she seems comfortable.*) Now let's review the retelling and look at the storybook to see how much you remembered. (*The teacher gives Beth the book and an evaluation form (see Figure 3.2) to evaluate her work.*)

After evaluating the retelling the following discussion occurred.

Beth: I have an introduction, "Once upon a time there was a girl named Jenny."

Teacher: Good, Beth, and you also named the main character and talked about her. Can you find that in your retelling?

Beth: (*Searching*) Yup, here it is.

The teacher and student move through the retelling and use the student assessment form as they find the elements included. They also note what is missing and comment on what to be careful about including when retelling the next story.

Practice, guidance, and evaluation of stories retold and rewritten have been found to improve children's written and oral original stories. In conferring with a student on original stories, the teacher can refer to the elements the child learned through retelling stories and can refer to the child's self-evaluation sheets to review the characteristics that make up a good story. Once children learn how to self-evaluate, they can do it independently and with their peers during center time. Figure 3.3 is a story evaluation form that can be used by both teachers and children.

Creative Storytelling Techniques

The teachers I worked with used creative techniques to make stories come alive. Such techniques excite the imagination, provide

FIGURE 3-2 Student Retelling Evaluation Form

Name_____ Date_____
Name of story_____

	Yes	No
Setting		
I began the story with an introduction.	____	____
I talked about the main character.	____	____
I talked about other characters.	____	____
I told when the story happened.	____	____
I told where the story happened.	____	____
Theme		
I told about the problem or the main goal of the characters.	____	____
Plot Episodes		
I included episodes in the story.	____	____
Resolution		
I told how the problem was solved.	____	____
I had an ending in the story.	____	____
Sequence		
My story was retold or rewritten in proper order.	____	____

Comments for Improvement
Next time I need to include in my retelling:

FIGURE 3-3   Story Evaluation Checklist

Name_____ Date_____
Name of story _____

	Yes	No
Setting		
The story begins with an introduction.	____	____
One or more main characters emerge.	____	____
Other characters are talked about.	____	____
The time of the story is mentioned.	____	____
Where the story takes place is mentioned.	____	____
Theme		
A beginning event occurs that causes a problem for the main character or a goal to be achieved.	____	____
The main character reacts to the problem.	____	____
Plot Episodes		
An event or series of events are mentioned that relate to the main character's solving the problem or attaining the goal.	____	____
Resolution		
The main character solves the problem or achieves the goal.	____	____
The story ends with a closing statement.	____	____
Sequence		
The four categories of story structure are presented in typical sequential order (setting, theme, plot episodes, resolution).	____	____

enjoyment to the listening audience, and, perhaps most important, get children interested in creating their own storytelling techniques. After telling a story to children, the actual book must be available, since children will be enticed to read and enjoy the book presented. Some stories are best told with no props; however, many lend themselves to the use of creative techniques. One can take cues from the content. When a story contains a good deal of dialogue, puppets may be suitable; other stories are perfect for felt board stories. Many stories are suited to several different techniques.

In Chapter 2, I described some materials for storytellers and how they were made. Here I will concentrate on how to use the techniques and what kinds of stories are appropriate for them. I began this chapter with descriptions of two teachers who were modeling creative techniques in their story readings. The first-grade teacher modeled the use of puppets with props when telling *The Very Hungry Caterpillar* (Carle 1970), and the fifth-grade teacher modeled the use of origami in teaching *Sadako and the Thousand Paper Cranes* (Coerr 1977). That is the best way to start: the teacher models the technique and then encourages the children to try it on their own. With children who are reading novels, they can select the part of the book they like best, they can summarize the story, tell about a chapter, describe the introduction, or create a symbol that characterizes the story. Older children create techniques as a form of book reporting and to entice their friends to read the book. Here are some techniques to use.

Felt Board Stories   As described in Chapter 2, stories can be told or read while placing felt characters on a felt board to provide a visual representation of the story. Stories that work best with the felt board have a limited number of characters that are introduced one at a time. The well-known folktale *The Mitten* (Brett 1989) is a good example of a felt board story. A small boy loses his mitten in the woods. Animals come one at a time and crawl into the mitten to stay warm. To tell the story with the felt board, first a large red felt mitten is placed on the board. As each animal is mentioned, its corresponding piece is placed on the red mitten. At the end of the story, the mitten is so full that it explodes and all of the animals come bursting out. To illustrate this, the teacher takes the red mitten off the felt board and shakes the animals onto the table. Children particularly enjoy this ending. Other books suitable for the felt board include *The Grouchy Ladybug* (Carle 1986) and *Tyrone the Horrible* (Wilhelm 1988). One fifth-grade teacher engaged her class in a felt board story with the book *Grandfather Tang's Story: A Tale Told with Tangrams* (Torbert 1990). She cut the tangram shapes from felt, and as the story was read in presentation to the class, the tangrams were assembled and reassembled on the felt board, as they took different forms of animals throughout the story.

Prop Stories Another storytelling technique is to use materials mentioned in the story to make it come to life. The props are displayed when needed. A fourth-grade teacher told the story *Gon Kitsune, a Fox Named Gon* (Nimi and Kuroi 1986), a Japanese folktale with a sad ending. To set the mood for the unusual experience his class was to encounter, the teacher draped a silk Japanese scarf across the front of his desk and decorated the desk top with Japanese artifacts. He put on a kimono, took off his shoes, and sat cross-legged on the desk to tell the story. This set the scene for his presentation. For *The Little Engine That Could* (Piper 1954), a kindergarten teacher collected some toy trains and toys to use at the right time in the story retelling.

Puppets Some classroom teachers have a storytelling puppet who tells stories to the children. For example, Mrs. Lettenberg had a special monkey puppet that the children named Chatter. The teacher is the only one who is allowed to use Chatter. He tells stories to the class. Other puppets that can be used for storytelling include stick puppets, finger puppets, and face puppets. This technique is especially useful in getting shy children to participate, since they are usually willing to hide behind a puppet when telling a story. Stories that work well with puppets are those with limited characters but a lot of conversation. Some good books for puppet presentations are *Amelia Bedelia* (Parish 1963), *William's Doll* (Zolotow 1972), and *Are You My Mother?* (Eastman 1960).

Chalk Talks The storyteller can draw the story on the chalkboard as it is told. It is best to preselect about five pictures of scenes from a book to draw for the chalk talk. As was mentioned in Chapter 2, the quality of the finished drawings is not important. The children will feel more secure in their own drawing if

Children use puppets to retell stories.

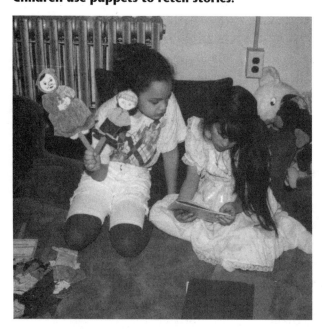

your artwork is less than perfect. The focus is on the telling of the story. Instead of a chalkboard, mural paper hung across a wall can be used; in this case, the storyteller uses crayons or felt-tip pens instead of chalk. When large boards or spaces are not available, a small easel can take their place. When drawing stories on an easel it is best to use sheets of paper that can be torn off easily to allow moving from one picture to the next. An overhead projector with a marker can also be used.

Some stories that make good chalk talks are *The Very Busy Spider* (Carle 1983) and the *Harold and the Purple Crayon* books (Johnson 1955). Teachers can use this technique with older children by having them introduce a chapter in a book or relating their favorite part of a book. Fables are good short stories for older students to chalk talk. One fifth-grade student did a chalk talk for a chapter in the book *My Side of the Mountain* (George 1959).

> 🎨 The resource section contains suggestions on using this book in a chalk talk (p. 152).

In addition to drawing different scenes from a story, chalk talks can have surprise endings. Here, a single picture is begun and added to as the story is told, with the completed picture the surprise at the end. The story *The Tale of the Black Cat* (Wither 1966) can be used as a chalk talk with a surprise ending; other titles are provided in the resource section. Once this type of chalk talk has been modeled for them, children in grades three through six can be asked to create their own.

Photo Stories Students can also become the characters in a book. A story that is easy to stage should be tried first; the teacher can help the children enact the main plot episodes. The enactment can be recorded with snapshots, which can be put into an album for the classroom library. A video recorder can also be used. Another alternative is to make a slide show with an audiotape made by the children. Good books for photo stories are *The*

Chalk talks help children retell stories.

Snowy Day (1962) and *A Letter to Amy* (1968), both by Ezra Jack Keats.

Sound Stories Sound stories are those in which the storyteller and the audience provide sound effects for a story while it is being told. The effects are often made with one's own voice. Rhythm instruments or some simple props can add to the presentation.

When preparing a sound story, the teacher should first select the places where sound effects will be used, then decide on the sound that will be made and who will make it. While the story is told the students chime in with their parts.

Sound stories can be recorded. The tape can be left in a listening center with earphones and the book. Children enjoy following the text of the book, the narration, and the sounds.

Many children's books are filled with references to sound. Good books for this technique are *Too Much Noise* (McGovern 1967) and *Mr. Brown Can Moo! Can You?* (Dr. Seuss 1970).

Music Stories Whether you can play an instrument or not, you can create a music story. Select a piece of literature with a limited number of well-delineated characters that appear throughout the story, such as *The Three Little Pigs* (Marshall 1989). If you can play an instrument, select a melody you know that seems appropriate for the character, and play that tune each time the character is mentioned in the story. Different tunes can be created to represent the different characters in the story.

Music can also be used as background. For example, older children can provide classical music to set the mood for novels, and scary sounds for mystery stories.

If you can't play an instrument, try using one anyway. For example, in the case of *The Three Little Pigs*, tinkle your fingers on the top high notes of a piano to represent the pigs and play this when they appear in the story. Pound slowly on the low bottom notes to represent the wolf. Roll your fists back and forth over a series of notes in the middle of the keyboard to represent the huffing and puffing of the big bad wolf. Slide your thumb from the top of the keyboard down to the bottom to represent the straw and stick houses falling down. Rhythm instruments also can be used for creating music stories by those with little or no training. In fact, often the most interesting music effects are developed in a music story by those who are not trained to play an instrument.

Music stories should always be tape recorded, especially when children participate. *The Three Billy Goats Gruff* (Brown 1957), *Goldilocks and the Three Bears* (Galdone 1972), and *The Little Red Hen* (Galdone 1975b) are good stories to set to music.

Roll Movie Stories   Roll movies were mentioned in Chapter 2. Again, the teacher should model the technique for children, with the goal of having them create roll stories themselves. Most younger students' books are appropriate for roll stories, as long as they have pictures that can be drawn by teachers. With older children's books, it is usually best to illustrate one chapter, or a favorite part of

the book, rather than the whole. For the book *Tuck Everlasting* (Babbitt 1975) a sixth grader used the prologue, which sets the scene for the book in a mysterious way with five situations. The student illustrated each of the five situations on shelving paper to create a roll movie to show classmates.

Cut Stories   With cut stories, the main character or characters are cut out in front of the audience while the story is being told. Usually the figures are drawn ahead of time on construction paper to make the cutting easier and to allow the teller to concentrate on telling the story. A quick and easy way to cut figures is to fold a piece of construction paper in half, draw half of the character on the folded paper, and then cut it out. Opening the folded paper reveals the entire figure.

It's a good idea for teachers to have on hand a few simple drawings of common characters and items—for example, a boy, a girl, a rabbit or other animals, a house, a tree, and so forth. These will be suitable for many stories. Good books for cut stories include the following:

- *Jean Marie Counts Her Sheep* (Charles 1951). Fold and draw half a sheep on eleven pieces of construction paper. As Jean Marie dreams of having each new sheep, cut out another and open it up.

- *The Carrot Seed* (Krauss 1945). Tell the whole story and at the end cut out the great big carrot that the little boy grew.

- *Miss Flora McFlimsey's Valentine* (Mariana 1962). Cut out the valentine.

Origami Stories   Origami, the art of Japanese paper folding, can be incorporated into storytelling. Many books on origami provide instruction on how to make various objects, including hats, flowers, fish, boats, and most animals. The most suitable kind of story for origami is one that focuses on one thing or character. While the story is told the paper is folded into the main character or object of the story, and when the story is over the object can be displayed. Older children are particularly attracted to this technique. They can be directed to books on the use of origami to help them create their stories. *The Happy Owls* (Piatti 1964) is a good story for origami, since the main characters are all owls, which can be created through paper folding. Other stories with characters that can be folded are as follows:

- *Jenny's Hat* (Keats 1966). Fold an origami hat, flowers, and birds.

- *The Lion and the Rat* (Wildsmith 1963) (a fable by LaFontaine). Fold an origami lion and rat.

The ultimate goal for the modeling of storytelling techniques is to have children use the materials the teacher has created to retell a story, create new materials for stories they read, and then create their own story and a technique to suit the theme.

> ✐ Additional book suggestions and directions for folding origami characters are provided in the resource section (pp. 179–183).

Literature Activities to Motivate Writing

Many of the activities for storytelling and retelling will stimulate children to write their own stories and books. Children can rewrite stories they have listened to. They can write their own original stories to use with the storytelling techniques such as a felt story, roll story, chalk talk, and so on. Series books, such as *Madeline* (Bemelmans 1977) for younger children or *Encyclopedia Brown* (Sobel 1970) for older children can stimulate students to write their own episode for the character. Popular television shows may also motivate children to write another episode for the program. Children write easily when they model their

stories and illustrations after those of authors with whom they are familiar.

Children are also motivated to write for functional reasons. If they are having a party in school, they will be happy to write invitations to parents or friends. A pen-pal arrangement with children in another school district can also motivate writing. Writing also occurs naturally in dramatic play that replicates real-life situations. For example, if the class is studying different cultures and the teacher has set up a restaurant to help students learn about different foods each week (one week Italian, then Japanese, Chinese, Greek, American, etc.), students will voluntarily write recipes, menus, checks, take reservations, and make signs for their restaurant.

Students learn skills as they participate in pleasurable reading and writing activities. By immersing themselves in literature activities, by reading and writing, they are practicing skills learned, as well as teaching and learning from each other, since the instructional setting provides for periods of reading and writing together. In the modeled lessons, teachers can include some skill development. Such skills as sequencing, interpreting, and predicting have already been demonstrated in most of the examples thus far provided. Word analysis can also be incorporated in storytelling and storybook reading. For example, when studying animals and reading stories such as *The Tale of Peter Rabbit* (Potter 1902), *The Pet Show* (Keats 1972), and *The Pig's Picnic* (Kasza 1988), the teacher can take the opportunity to explain the sound of the letter *P*. Thus, in addition to their being enjoyable, such experiences with literature also teach children skills.

Reading and Writing Across the Curriculum

Reading, writing, and oral language materials and activities are easily incorporated into content instruction, enabling these areas to contribute to literacy learning. Literacy becomes purposeful and takes on additional importance when integrated with other content areas (Dewey 1966).

Subject-specific literacy materials will be found in content areas throughout the classroom, including books, magazines and newspapers for children to read, materials with which they may write, and activities they can talk about and do. These materials create interest, new vocabulary, and ideas, and in general a reason for participating in literacy activities. With each new theme studied, additional books, posters, artifacts, music, art projects, dramatic play materials, and scientific objects are added to create new interest.

Themes help to motivate reading and writing, since the topics chosen are of interest to children. Content area materials should be coordinated with themes. For example, Mrs. Mitchell's third-grade class carried out an extended study of plants (Rand 1994). As a science activity the class used a "Do-It-Yourself Science" book called *All About Seeds* (Berger 1992) to carry out experiments about what plants need to grow. They planted seeds, withholding water, soil, and warmth in various combinations and making predictions about the growth of the seeds. Each day they wrote their observations in the class science journal.

Other activities grew out of the plant topic. A gardening center was set up to make a window box garden for the classroom. The class referred to the book *Kids Gardening* (Raferty 1989) as a resource for how to prepare the soil, what seeds to plant, and how to care for them. Mrs. Mitchell also read a story to the class about the rain forest. In this story the treasures of the rain forest, along with the dangers of deforestation, are discovered and discussed. The children created a large mural to show the types of plants and animals that live in the rain forest. To find out what was appropriate to include, they used informational books such as *Rain Forest Secrets* (Dorros 1990) and *Life in the Rain Forests* (Baker 1990), which were

placed in the art area. As a final project, the class wrote a letter to their congressional representative to voice their ideas and concerns. Mrs. Mitchell took this opportunity to teach the children the form of a business letter. During literacy center time, Tara wrote a story about what the world would be like if there were no more rain forests. She titled her book *The Day the Forest Died*. After the final editing was done, the book was published and became part of the classroom library collection.

In another third-grade class that was involved in science, where the teacher integrated literature with content area teaching, it was difficult to determine whether what was going on was a literacy lesson or a science lesson. The class had just completed a unit on animals and was about to begin one on "The Changing Earth." When the science period began, Ms. Scifflette, the teacher, called the children to the literacy center. They sat on the rug and Ms. Scifflette sat in the rocking chair. With her she had the rack that held the science trade books. It was filled with stories about animals. She said, "Since we have completed our animal unit I will put these books in the science section of our classroom library. I'm going to change the sign on the science book rack to 'The Changing Earth,' since that is our next topic." She asked the children if they could predict what they might be studying about with the topic "The Changing Earth." Dominick said, "Maybe how the rocks change from years of wind and rain on them." Ms. Scifflette agreed that was a good idea. Stacey said, "Hurricanes can change the earth when they blow down trees and wash away the sand from the beach." Ms. Scifflette agreed with her about that. She then introduced five books and read their titles: *Volcanoes* (Branley 1985), *How to Dig a Hole to the Other Side of the World* (McNulty 1979), *Time of Wonder* (McCloskey 1957), *The Magic School Bus Inside the Earth* (Cole 1987), and *Bringing the Rains to Kapiti Plain* (Aardema 1981). She explained that these stories, along with their textbook, would help them learn about the changing earth. She said that she'd be reading them during the unit and that she would leave them in the special featured science book rack for them to read during their free time. She asked if anyone had any more ideas about what "The Changing Earth" unit might be about as a result of hearing these book titles. Tiffany said, "I guess volcanoes, since they change the earth with all that hot stuff that pours out of them." Tim added, "We're probably gonna learn about what's inside the earth, from the titles of those books you told us about." "I know that *Bringing the Rains to Kapiti Plain* is about drought," said Alex. "The dry land causes the ground to change."

Ms. Scifflette was teaching science and at the same heightening her students' interest about the topic to be studied through the use of children's literature.

Later, after they had been studying "The Changing Earth" for a while, the class assembled in the literacy center for the science lesson. The teacher sat in the rocking chair while the children sat on the rug. Ms. Scifflette picked up a book about the changing earth and wrote the title on a chart: *How to Dig a Hole to the Other Side of the World* (McNulty 1979). She underlined the title and asked the children why she had done that. Bernice replied, "When you write the name of a book, you are supposed to underline it." "Good," said Ms. Scifflette. She continued, "We've been studying the changing earth and what the earth is made up of. This book is factual and it also has fictional information. While I'm reading, try to remember the facts we come across. After I finish we'll record those facts. After that we'll retell the story together, and emphasize the facts." Ms. Scifflette read the name of the author and illustrator and began the story. After reading, the class discussed the facts and Ms. Scifflette wrote them on the chart. This discussion followed.

"What is the first thing that you hit when you dig a hole in the earth?" the teacher asked. Tyrone replied, "Loam. It is like topsoil. Then we could find clay." "Good," said Ms.

Scifflette. "Then what?" Adelise raised her hand: "Next comes bones, rock, and limestone." Joseph asked, "Isn't rock the same as limestone?" "Yes," replied Ms. Scifflette. "Now what do we find?" The children responded together, "Crust and then water." "What else?" asked Ms. Scifflette. Kevin answered, "I think oil is next. I guess that's what people mean by 'filthy rich.' When you find oil you get rich, but you also get dirty from digging." "There are geysers with scalding hot water and basalt. Who can tell me more about basalt?" asked Ms. Scifflette. Tyshone raised his hand. "Well, when it's in the earth it is black, and when it is melted it is called magma. When it comes out of the earth through volcanoes, then it's called lava." Jennifer raised her hand. "The next part is fictional, the book talked about going through the layers of the earth in a jet-propelled red submarine." "Good. I'm glad you can tell the difference," said Ms. Scifflette. "Who can finish up?" Damien and Dan continued, back and forth, "Well next they came to mantel, which is hot." Ms. Scifflette wrote that on the chart. "Then there is the outer core made of melted rock and iron and the inner core at the center of the earth. After the center he goes back through all the other stuff again till he came out on the other side." Ms. Scifflette said, "That was great. Now would someone retell the entire story with the facts listed on the chart?" April volunteered and began with "Once upon a time there was a boy who wanted to dig a hole to the other side of the world." She followed the facts on the chart to the end. When she finished, everyone clapped.

Encouraging writing about science topics was also stressed in these integrated language arts classrooms. For example, Ms. Scifflette's class would brainstorm words about topics being studied by filling in a web entitled "What Changes the Earth?" Using the words generated by the web, such as hurricane, volcano, lava, drought, and so forth, children wrote stories about the science theme (see Figure 3.4). Some students found this activity dif-

FIGURE 3-4   Story Web

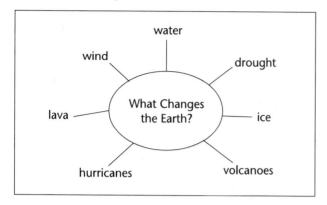

ficult at first, but after a while they got the idea. They wrote their science stories and used many of the storytelling techniques outlined earlier in this chapter to present them to the class.

After a brainstorming session about vocabulary and concepts related to the changing earth, Ms. Scifflette guided her students as they wrote a class story.

The Treasure Hunt

My friends Amber, Alex, and Kevin found a map of a buried treasure. We decided to look for it. We followed the map to hunt for the treasure. It said go to a stream and find waters that get rough that made the rocks strange shapes from banging up against them. We walked for hours and then Kevin shouted, "Look, there are the rocks." We looked for the next clue. Amber found it carved in the rock. It was hard to read from the wear of the wind and water. It said, "Go to the forest and find the clearing with the colored flowers." We walked for hours. It was hot and dry, the ground was hard, it hadn't rained for months, the grass was brown, the flowers were dead with no color in them from the drought. Then the sky got dark, the wind blew 100 miles an hour, the rain came down in buckets, we ran into a cave. This was a hurricane. When the storm ended it looked like a different place. Trees fell, the lake washed away the beach, but

colored flowers were growing. We had found the spot. We saw a note that said go to the mountain. We saw it ahead. We ran toward it. The earth began to shake, the mountain rumbled. It wasn't a mountain, it was a volcano. Red hot lava ran down the side. We ran for cover. When the volcano finished erupting the earth was covered with ash. When it was safe we came out to look for a clue. I saw a paper. It said go to the forest and you will find it. When we got there, the leaves were green, the flowers were pretty, the sky was blue, there was a breeze, there was fruit to eat on the trees and birds were singing and the sun was warm. Alex said, "This is it." "What?" we said. Alex said, "We saw changes in the earth that were scary like jagged rocks from wind and water, and a hurricane that blew down trees, and a volcano burned up the ground. Now we can see the beautiful part of the earth. This is the treasure." We all agreed and enjoyed the pretty earth.

In a first-grade classroom that was using an integrated language arts approach to motivate reading and writing in content subjects, the teacher, Mr. Gravois, extended the theme—the study of animals—to all the learning areas in the classroom. To encourage literacy skill development, Mr. Gravois added the following materials and activities for students to participate in at each of the centers.

Art Center Printed directions for making play dough were written on a chart for the art center. After following these directions, and making the modeling clay, children created real or imaginary animals for a pretend zoo they designed in the block area. The children named their animals and wrote their names on index cards as they placed them in the zoo. This center encouraged skill development: the children had to use their knowledge about print when they read the recipe for the play dough. They also practiced sound-symbol relationships when writing the animal names on index cards. They improved their skills at their own level in a functional context as they voluntarily engaged in reading and writing.

Music Center Children sang animal songs and Mr. Gravois wrote the words to new songs on chart paper that was displayed in the music center. The teacher encouraged the children to read or copy the charts. In the music center, skills in vocabulary development were enhanced and the relationship between oral and written language was strengthened.

Science Center Mr. Gravois borrowed a hen whose eggs were ready to hatch. The class discussed the care of the hen. They started an experience chart when the hen arrived and added to it daily, recording the hen's behavior and the hatching of the eggs. They listed new vocabulary words on a wall chart and placed books about hens in the science area. Children kept journals of events concerning the hen. Index cards were available in the center for children to record new "Very Own Words" relating to the hen. The science center was rich in opportunities for children to develop early writing, vocabulary, and sight words.

Social Studies Center Pictures of animals from different countries were placed in the social studies area along with a map highlighting where they come from. Children could match the animals to the appropriate place on the map. They also made their own books about animals around the world. During center time, Mr. Gravois helped some children identify beginning sounds by writing the animal names for them in their books. He worked with other children who could already write conventionally to help them focus on the mechanical skills of writing, such as the use of capitalization and punctuation.

Math Center Counting books that feature animals, such as *Count!* (Fleming 1992) and *One, Two, Three, to the Zoo* (Carle 1968), were placed in the math center along with math manipulatives such as Unifix cubes. The children developed both math and literacy skills by matching the appropriate amount of manipulatives to the number names and number symbols in the books.

Dramatic Play Center The dramatic play area became a pet store. There were (empty) boxes of pet food and other products for animals, all marked with prices. A pet supply checklist was available for customers to decide what things they needed and how much they would cost. There were sales slips for writing orders, receipts for purchases made, and a calculator to help figure totals. Animal magazines and pamphlets that discussed pet care were present in the store, and pet posters labeled with animals' names were hanging on the walls. Other materials included a sign that said "OPEN" and "CLOSED," with store hours posted as well. Stuffed animals were used as the pets for sale. They were placed in boxes that served as cages, labeled with the animals' names. There were appointment cards for grooming pets and a checklist for owners to record activities necessary for maintaining a healthy pet. The environmental print and writing materials in this center provided the children a chance to practice literacy skills in a meaningful way.

Block Play Center The block area became a zoo, housing animal figures, stuffed animals, and play dough animals created by the children in the art center. Children used the blocks to create cages and made labels and signs for each animal and section of the zoo, such as "Petting Zoo," "Bird House," "Pony Rides," "Don't Feed the Animals," and "Don't Touch Us, We Bite." There were admission tickets and play money to purchase tickets and souvenirs. In many classrooms, literacy materials are not found in the block corner, but the simple addition of markers, paper, and index cards resulted in children's participation in writing activities.

Literacy Center Books and magazines about animals were highlighted on the open-faced bookshelves of the literacy center. The author's spot had animal-shaped blank books for writing animal stories. Many of the activities from other centers spread into the literacy center, and it became a central resource for information and materials.

The School Library or Media Center

The school librarian or media specialist is a valuable resource in establishing a program for self-directed and collaborative literature experiences (see Lamme and Ledbetter, 1990 for many suggestions). The most obvious role the librarian can play is as a guide to select books for the classroom library, since he or she will be most familiar with the current literature and can also gauge the likely popularity of books. Librarians can also give presentations to update teachers and students about new literature. In addition, they can help coordinate read-aloud book lists for different grade levels to ensure that students will be exposed to a wide variety of literature as they progress in school.

The librarian is also a resource for children's learning to read and tell stories. He or she can serve as a role model for classroom teachers and can also conduct workshops on storytelling, puppet making, and reading aloud, and can visit classrooms to read to children. The librarian can help set up the coding system for books in classroom libraries. He or she can make connections for the children between the classroom and the school library collections and coding systems. In an ideal situation, the librarian can coordinate schoolwide thematic units and keep on file units

completed. These units would contain activity plans, teaching strategies, and extensive lists of annotated bibliographies of children's literature for classroom use.

The Role of Parents

In Chapter 1 we discussed literacy-rich home environments where children learned to read without direct instruction. These children were motivated to read and write by parents who provided a model for reading and writing, by doing so themselves in their daily lives. Parents read to children and discussed issues related to literacy in their daily routines. These parents also provided materials in the home for children to read and write with—books, magazines, and newspapers in many rooms of the home for adults and children; writing materials, from pencils to markers; and paper of many sizes and shapes. In addition to parents providing rich literacy environments at home, they must also be an integral part of the child's education at school. Teachers should provide parents with a list of things to do with their child at home (see Figure 3.5) and include parents in the child's school activities. Parents also need a list of activities that happen in school, and they should be invited to school to read to the children, to help bind books, and to participate generally in literacy center time. Parents from diverse backgrounds can share books from their culture and stories read and told to them as children. Teachers should invite parents to meetings to discuss the role families play in literacy development at home and in school. In short, once children are in school, parents should take an active role in their education, to support the school's efforts. Parents' motivating literacy activities at home and coming to school to take part in literacy center time will make a strong impact on their children. The children will associate working

FIGURE 3-5 Guidelines for Promoting Early Literacy at Home

Your youngster's ability to read and write depends a lot on the things you do at home from the time he or she is born. You can do many things to help that will not take much of your time. The following list suggests materials, activities, and attitudes that are important in helping your child learn to read and write. Check off the things you already do. Try and do something on the list that you haven't done before.

Materials
❑ 1. Have a space at home for books and magazines for your child.
❑ 2. If you can, subscribe to a magazine for your child.
❑ 3. Place some of your child's and some of your books, magazines, and newspapers in different parts of your home.
❑ 4. Provide materials that will encourage children to tell or create their own stories, such as puppets, dolls, and story tapes.
❑ 5. Provide materials for writing, such as crayons, markers, pencils, and paper in different sizes.

Activities
❑ 1. Read or look at books, magazines, or the newspaper with your child. Talk about what you looked at or read.
❑ 2. Visit the library and take out books and magazines to read at home.
❑ 3. Tell stories together about books, about your family, and about things that you do.
❑ 4. Look at and talk about written material you have, such as catalogues, advertisements, work-related materials, and mail.
❑ 5. Provide a model for your child by reading and writing at a time when they can see you.
❑ 6. Point to print outside, such as road signs and names of stores.
❑ 7. Write with your child and talk about what you write.
❑ 8. Point out print in your home, such as words on food boxes, recipes, directions on medicine, or things to put together.
❑ 9. Visit the post office, supermarket, or zoo. Talk about what you saw and read. When you get home, draw and write about it.
❑ 10. Use print to talk to your child. Leave notes for each other; make lists of things to do, such as food lists, lists of errands, and lists for holiday shopping.

Fostering Positive Attitudes Toward Reading and Writing
❑ 1. Reward your child's attempts at reading and writing, even if they aren't perfect, by offering praise. Say kind words like: "What nice work you do." "I'm happy to see you reading." "I'm happy to see you writing." "Can I help you?"
❑ 2. Answer your child's questions about reading and writing.
❑ 3. Be sure that reading and writing are enjoyable experiences.
❑ 4. Display children's work in your home.
❑ 5. Visit school when your child asks. Volunteer to help at school, attend programs in which your child is participating, attend parent conferences, attend parent meetings. This lets your child know you care about him or her and school.

Visit School and Speak to Your Child's Teacher
❑ 1. If you want to volunteer to help in any way.
❑ 2. If you want to visit your child's class during school hours.
❑ 3. If you have concerns about your child's reading and writing.
❑ 4. If you feel your child has any special problems with his or her vision, hearing, or other things.
❑ 5. If you need help because the language you speak at home is not English.
❑ 6. If you need help with reading and writing yourself.
❑ 7. If you'd like to know more about how you can help your child at home.
❑ 8. If you want to know more about and understand better what your child is learning at school.

with their parents as a pleasurable activity and transfer that association to reading and writing in school. A form soliciting parent participation in literacy center time can be used to encourage parents to come to school and be a part of their children's education (see Figure 3.6).

An Activities Checklist

The resource section contains several sample activities for teachers to model during literacy center time. These lessons are based on activities teachers have provided for children

FIGURE 3-6 Sample of Invitation to Parents for Literacy Center Time

HELP WANTED   HELP WANTED   HELP WANTED   HELP WANTED

Dear Families,

   We want to invite you to come to school to participate in our literacy center time. This is a time where children read and write together, choosing materials and activities they would like to do. We want you to read and write with them, and you can take part in many ways. Below is a form listing the types of things you could do during literacy center time and a space for you to let us know the time of day and date that you can attend. We are flexible and will arrange our time for literacy center activities when it is convenient for you to come. After you visit once you will want to come again, and we want you to come as often as possible. All family members are welcome—younger brothers and sisters, babies, aunts, uncles, grandparents, and friends as well as parents.

   Please come, get involved in your child's education, and help us form a true home and school partnership.

   Sincerely,
   Mrs. Tofel and her fourth-grade class

Please fill out the following form and send it back to school with your child.

Come and Visit School During Literacy Center Time
Your name _____
Your child's name _____
The days I can come during the week are _____.
The time of day I can come to school is _____.

When I come to school I would like to do the following:
   1. Just watch what the children are doing._____
   2. Participate with the children in literacy center time. _____
   3. Read to a small group of children._____
   4. Read to the whole class._____
   5. I am from another country and I would like to tell the children about my country and show them clothing, pictures, and books from there._____
   6. I have a hobby and would like to share it with the class.
      My hobby is_____.
   7. I have a talent and I would like to share it with the class.
      My talent is_____.
   8. I'd like to tell the children about my job. My job is _____.
   9. Other ideas you would like to do?_____
   10. I don't know what to do. _____

that have been found to motivate them to read and write. They include ideas for storytelling, teaching skills in pleasurable ways, and integrating reading and writing into content areas. In addition, Figure 3.7 on the next page provides a summary of literature activities. Teachers can use this form as a checklist of activities already being pursued and as suggestions of what could be incorporated into the classroom. All of the activities children can do either in collaboration with other children or alone.

Parents are invited to come to the literacy center and participate with children.

FIGURE 3-7 Literature Activities Modeled and Initiated by Teachers

Check the activities you have already tried in the classroom, and consider trying the others.

- ❑ 1. Read and tell stories to children.
- ❑ 2. Discuss stories read in many different ways.
- ❑ 3. Have a 30-minute literacy center period three to five times a week that includes the use of books and all other literature-related materials in the library corner.
- ❑ 4. During literacy center time, model reading.
- ❑ 5. Allow children to check out books from the classroom library.
- ❑ 6. Encourage children to read during their spare time.
- ❑ 7. Have children keep track of books read.
- ❑ 8. Have children keep the literacy center orderly.
- ❑ 9. Read poetry to the children.
- ❑ 10. Have the class recite poetry.
- ❑ 11. Use part of a reading period for sharing books read at home or at school.
- ❑ 12. Have the principal, custodian, nurse, secretary, or a parent read to the children.
- ❑ 13. Discuss authors and illustrators.
- ❑ 14. Write to authors.
- ❑ 15. Have children read to younger children.
- ❑ 16. Have children read to each other.
- ❑ 17. Show filmstrips or movies of stories.
- ❑ 18. Use literature across the curriculum in content-area lessons.
- ❑ 19. Relate art activities to books (e.g., draw a mural related to a book or create a picture using the technique of a particular illustrator of children's books).
- ❑ 20. Tell stories using a creative storytelling technique such as:

    a. felt boards   e. music stories
    b. roll movies   f. chalk stories
    c. puppets   g. prop stories
    d. sound stories   h. cut stories

- ❑ 21. Have children tell stories with and without props.
- ❑ 22. Have children act out stories.
- ❑ 23. Prepare recipes related to stories (e.g., make stone soup after reading the story of the same name).
- ❑ 24. Read TV-related stories.
- ❑ 25. Make class books and "very own books," bind them, and store them in the library corner.
- ❑ 26. Sing songs that have been made into books and have the book on hand (e.g., "I Know an Old Lady Who Swallowed a Fly").
- ❑ 27. Make bulletin boards related to books.
- ❑ 28. Have children write advertisements for good books they have read.
- ❑ 29. Discuss the proper way to care for and handle books.
- ❑ 30. Feature new books in the open-faced bookshelves.
- ❑ 31. Introduce new books on the open-faced bookshelves.
- ❑ 32. Introduce new books in the literacy corner.
- ❑ 33. Circulate 25 new books every two weeks.
- ❑ 34. Provide booklets for children and parents for selecting books to read in and out of school.
- ❑ 35. Have a bookstore in the school where children can buy books regularly.
- ❑ 36. Give bookmarks to children.
- ❑ 37. Give each child a book as a gift.
- ❑ 38. Have a young authors' conference (share books children have written, bind books, invite authors).
- ❑ 39. Have a book fair for children to purchase books.
- ❑ 40. Have a book celebration day (dress up as book characters, tell stories to each other, show movie and filmstrip stories, have stories told creatively, etc.).
- ❑ 41. Take a field trip related to books (e.g., book binding factory, town library, publishing company).
- ❑ 42. Have children order books from a book club.
- ❑ 43. Provide a newsletter a few times a year about book-related activities in school.
- ❑ 44. Ask parents to participate in some literature-related activity at school (e.g., reading with children, helping with book binding, raising money to buy books, participating in literacy center time at school).
- ❑ 45. Have a workshop for parents that describes the importance, purpose, and activities of the school literature program.
- ❑ 46. Have a workshop for parents describing how they can participate in a home recreational reading program.

Using the Literacy Center: Organization, Management, and Assessment

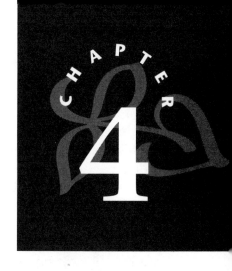

In Mrs. Thaxton's third grade the children are engaged in literacy center time. The teacher has reviewed the choices of activities and decided that the emphasis for the day would be to read traditional tales, those handed down over the years from one group of people to the next. Among the books the class discussed were *Little Red Riding Hood* (Grimm Brothers 1968), *The Gingerbread Boy* (Galdone 1975a), and *The Three Billy Goats Gruff* (Asbojornsen and Jorgen 1957). Children were to compare the themes of the story to see the similarities in style. Mrs. Thaxton asked the children to form groups and make a decision about what they would do. They would record their decision on a sign-up sheet before going off to work together. The students knew that during this period they would be working on something for which there needed to be an outcome or performance for their classmates. Children could choose to read an original folktale they had written, tell about the different versions of a particular folktale, do a felt story presentation about a story read, or whatever else they could think of that was related to the idea of traditional tales. They would have about a week to complete their project, depending on the progress made.

Once the children had made choices concerning with whom they would work and what they would do, they began their activities.

John and Tasha were reading several different versions of *The Three Little Pigs* (Brenner 1972) as they relaxed on soft pillows, both holding stuffed animals as they read. When they finished reading, they discussed the differences between the versions. Christopher read to James while the two of them were inside the box called the private spot. Jacki and Jerome used a felt board to tell the story *The Three Billy Goats Gruff* (Asbojornsen and Jorgen 1957). One manipulated the felt characters as the other read the book. A group listened to a taped story of *The Little Red Hen* (Galdone 1975b) on headsets. They followed the words in the book as they listened. Since the tape was audible only to children with headsets, it was amusing to hear them chanting along at the part in the story when the animals respond ("'Not I,' said the dog," etc.).

Tyrone and Jessy were writing letters to their pen pals about their work with fairy tales. They and their pen pals' classrooms had coordinated programs: the two classes were working on the same project so the students could correspond about their work in common. A few children were checking out books to take home, and others were looking in their logs, comparing the number of books they had read and the literacy tasks they had accomplished. Elvira pretended to be the teacher and gathered a group of children around her as she sat in the rocking chair and read a story to them.

At the beginning of the period Mrs. Thaxton walked around to make sure that children were involved. She helped a group that was having difficulty getting started on a roll movie they wanted to create for the story of *Cinderella* (Perrault 1954). Then she observed a few youngsters acting out *The Three Bears and Fifteen Other Stories* (Rockwell 1984) with finger puppets. After that she sat down with a novel and read, modeling her own interest in books. The room was generally quiet, but one could hear the buzz of activity. Not only were the children's activities productive, they were also relevant—each child or group of children had interpreted for themselves the concept to be focused on during this independent reading and writing period. All were doing different activities, but all were using folk and fairy tales.

Literacy centers are especially useful because they provide students with opportunities for collaborative learning and the elements that promote motivation for reading and writing. But what are the benefits of cooperative and collaborative learning experiences, as described in the vignette above? What types of cooperative and collaborative settings can children be involved in? And how does a teacher organize and manage a collabo-

When all the children were settled into literacy center time activities, Mrs. Thaxton sat among them with a novel and read, modeling her own interest in books.

rative literacy setting—the literacy center—where children work productively in social groups, independent of the teacher?

Benefits of Cooperative and Collaborative Learning Experiences

The aim of cooperative learning is to bring children together so they can teach and learn from each other through discussion and debate. Social interaction and collaboration within small groups of children promotes achievement and productivity (Johnson et al. 1981; Slavin 1983). According to researchers, cooperative learning succeeds because it allows children to explain material to each

other, to listen to each others' explanations, and to arrive at a joint understanding of what has been shared. In the cooperative setting, more capable peers support others in the group. For example, they may observe, guide, and correct while the others perform a particular task (Forman and Cazden 1985). The students are able to accomplish together what they could not do alone. Such peer interaction offers the same learning opportunities as tutoring.

In cooperative settings children form friendships and develop greater acceptance of differences. High and low achievers are able to work together, as are children from varied racial and ethnic backgrounds. Children with special needs (physical disabilities, emotional handicaps, learning difficulties) and social isolates are more likely to be accepted in cooperative learning settings than in traditional classroom structures. (See Augustine, Gruber, and Hanson 1989; Johnson and Johnson 1987; Kagan et al. 1985; Lew et al. 1986; Slavin 1990.)

Cooperative Learning Settings

Several models for cooperative learning have been developed that are adaptable for most grade levels and subjects. In general, cooperative learning occurs in groups in which student members work together to achieve a common goal (Slavin 1985). Some settings are quite structured; others leave considerable room for choice on the part of the children.

Student Team Learning

One of the more structured forms of cooperative learning is student team learning (Slavin 1990). Students are assigned to four-member teams, with each team mixed in ability, ethnicity, and sex. The teacher presents a lesson, then students work in teams to help all members master the lesson. Students take individual tests, and their performance is compared with their past scores. Points are awarded based on the degree to which students have met or exceeded earlier scores. Individual students' points are added up to get a team score. Teams that meet certain criteria are rewarded.

Group Investigation

Group investigation is another cooperative learning strategy in which students form their own groups of two to six members. After choosing topics from a unit being studied by the entire class, the groups break their topics

into individual tasks, which will ultimately be combined into group reports. Reports can be in several forms, such as a demonstration, a play, or an exhibit for the class. Evaluation focuses on both learning and on children's attitudes about what they are doing. Assessment may include peer comments, self-evaluations, questions from the group, and teacher evaluation (Sharan and Sharan 1989–90).

Learning Together

Another cooperative method is known as "learning together." Students work on assignments in heterogeneous groups of four or five members. The emphasis is on building social skills for successful group work—developing trust, communicating accurately and straightforwardly, accepting and supporting group members, and resolving conflicts constructively. Each group completes a single product and is praised for the ability of its members to work together as well as for the quality of the group's performance (Johnson and Johnson 1987).

The literacy center is similar to the group investigation and learning together settings described above. Since it has been found that choice increases productivity during literacy activity (Graves 1975), it is important that social settings allow for student choice, both in task selection and in group membership. The goal is for students to complete activities successfully while learning to work together.

Collaborative Literacy Settings

There are several configurations for collaboration in the classroom. The most productive are those in which the children are responsible for working together and accomplishing tasks independent of the teacher. Such settings include the following.

Buddy Reading and Writing

Buddy reading and writing, as the term suggests, involves pairing a child from an upper grade with a child in kindergarten, first, or second grade. The child in the upper grade is given instruction on how to read to children and participate in other literacy activities as well. With their teacher, the older students plan activities for each buddy reading and writing session. At specified times during the week the buddies get together for reading and writing. Both the older and younger child benefit from these interactions. The younger child's literacy is enhanced from the mentoring he or she is receiving. The older child is learning how to teach, discovering in the process that the teacher often learns as much as the student. Wonderful social relationships are also formed in this learning structure.

Partner reading and writing involves peers who are paired by the teacher or by their own choice for reading and writing activities.

Although partner reading and writing typically includes students with similar skills, it can also pair a more capable child with one who could benefit from peer tutoring.

Partner Reading and Writing

Partner reading and writing, like the buddy system, involves pairs of students, but in this case the pairs are peers from the same class who have been chosen either by the teacher or by themselves for the purpose of reading and writing together. Activity sheets guide the students, helping them know how to proceed. Questions that prompt aesthetic conversation about texts can be used (see Chapter 3). A typical project for partner reading and writing is as follows.

1. Select and read a book of your choice.

2. Discuss the part you both liked best and write it down.

3. Prepare a roll story illustrating the parts you discussed.

Literature Circles

Literature circles can be formed for children to discuss books they have read. Children can discuss the same book or different ones. Teachers need to model literature circle activities in order for students then to carry them out successfully. The teacher needs to begin by leading the discussion in the circles. Then, when the children understand how literature circles operate, they can carry them out on their own. A set of questions for discussion, adjusted by grade level, can help make the circle conversations productive. (Questions that motivate engaged discussion can be found in Chapter 3.)

Children can be given different roles in the literature circle, such as the leader, who organizes who will speak when, and the recorder, who writes down important responses. In addition, students can be assigned specific questions to pose to others. Harvey Daniels' book *Literature Circles* (1994) provides useful information about this form of collaboration.

Writing Conferences

Writing conferences can be held between teachers and students and between students themselves. During peer conferences, children share pieces of their own writing for the purpose of seeking guidance. Teachers need to provide a model for helping children discuss their writing constructively and in a supportive manner. Questions for discussion can help make the conference productive, such as:

- What are the good points about the piece of writing?

- What could be improved? For example:
  Is the setting stated?
  Is there a main character?
  Does the main character have a problem to solve or a goal to achieve?
  Are there episodes that help the main character solve the problem or attain the goal?
  Does the story end with a resolution to the problem or attainment of the goal?
  Is there an end to the story?

Teacher-Guided Conference Periods

Teachers can work with small groups of children or one child at a time for guided instruction. For this to happen, children must be working on their own, alone or in social settings independent of the teacher. While the teacher is involved with one child or group, the others continue their independent work. The literacy center activities suggested in this book reflect the type of work children can engage in independently during teacher-guided conference periods.

General Center Time

Students can work independent of the teacher in different areas of the classroom designated for specific subjects, such as science, social studies, art, and math as well as literacy. Children can choose which area to go to and what they will do when they get there. Of course, as stressed throughout the book, literacy activities need to be a part of every subject area.

Reading and Writing Workshop

A workshop setting for reading and writing, as described by Don Graves (1983) and Lucy Calkins (1986), among others, is similar to the literacy center time described in this book. Often the teacher conducts a whole-group lesson or "minilesson" on a specific skill, and the children may then practice that skill in the workshop setting, among themselves and independent of the teacher (Atwell 1987).

Literacy Center Time

During literacy center time teachers model an activity or skill, and then children select whom they will work with. When groups are formed, children select what tasks they will undertake. They share what they have accomplished when the activities are completed. Literacy center time can be used to reinforce skills learned while encouraging pleasurable participation in reading and writing activities.

During literacy center time children can *choose* from several different literacy activities on which to work, either alone or with others; *observe* literacy behaviors while being read to or seeing peers and teachers engaged in similar activities; *collaborate* with peers and be supported by more literate others; *practice* what has been learned in more traditional settings;

and *perform* literacy accomplishments by sharing reading and writing projects with peers and adults.

In Chapter 2, I outlined how to design a classroom literacy center, and in Chapter 3, I suggested pleasurable, teacher-modeled, skill-oriented literacy activities that can motivate students to read and write. In the remainder of this chapter I discuss the organization and management of literacy center time.

Organizing and Managing Collaborative Literacy Settings

Collaborative learning is meant to take place within a total school program that also provides students with more traditional explicit instruction as well. The social setting for literacy activities is not meant to be a steady diet throughout the school day. In addition, the guidelines I suggest for managing such programs should be generalized to the specific teaching situation and modified for the teacher's individual needs. Regardless of the setting used, children need to know (1) the choices they have for activities to participate in, (2) rules that guide participation concerning the selection of materials and groups, and what is to happen in those groups, (3) guidelines for cooperating, and (4) expectations for outcomes as a result of participating in the groups. Cooperative settings require a strong underlying structure that provides the student with freedom within limits.

Literacy center time is carried out from three to five times a week for thirty to forty-five minutes. During each period children are given the opportunity to decide what they will do and whom they will work with. Most periods, or at least portions of them, focus on a literacy skill to be developed or a content area theme being studied. If children are

FIGURE 4-1 Guidelines to Follow During Literacy Center Time

1. Decide whom you will work with or if you will work alone.
2. Choose a reading or writing activity.
3. Do only one or two activities in a period.
4. Materials can be used in or outside of the literacy center.
5. Be sure that what you do includes reading and writing.
6. Handle the materials carefully.
7. Speak in soft voices—people are working.
8. Put materials back in their place before taking another.
9. Try activities you haven't done before.
10. Try working with people you haven't worked with before.
11. Be ready to share your completed tasks with the class.
12. Record completed activities in your log.
13. Keep the literacy center neat.

learning about animals in science, for example, they may be asked to focus their collaborative reading and writing activities on this topic. Similarly, if the teacher has emphasized character study during storybook reading, the children might be asked to focus on qualities of characters they read or write about during literacy center time.

Learning How to Work in Groups

The guidelines for children to follow during literacy center time are posted and reviewed before each session (see Figure 4.1). In addition to rules pertaining to the use of materials, children are taught cooperative skills; these are also posted (see Figure 4.2). Included in the list of aids to cooperative behavior are helpful things children can say to each other, helpful things they can do for

FIGURE 4-2 Rules for Cooperating During Literacy Center Time

Helpful Things to Do When Working in Groups

Select a leader to help the group get started.

Select a recorder to write down what the group does.

Select a reporter to share the accomplishments of the group.

Give everyone a job.

Take turns talking.

Share materials.

Listen to your friends when they talk.

Stay with your group.

Helpful Things to Say When Working in Groups

Can I help you?

I like your work.

You did a good job.

Check Your Work

Did you say helpful things?

Did you help each other?

Did you share materials?

Did you take turns?

Did you all have jobs?

How well did your jobs get done?

What can we do better next time?

each other, and directions for selecting leaders, designating assignments to members of the group, and evaluating cooperative behavior and the completion of tasks.

Both sets of guidelines can be printed on colored sheets of paper, laminated, and displayed in the literacy centers for students to refer to.

Selection of Groups and Activities

When literacy center time begins, some teachers assign children to groups and decide which activities they will participate in; other teachers assign children to groups and allow them to decide on the task they would like to do together; others outline activities that can be done and have children form groups based on the activity they would like to do; and still others allow children to decide whom they would like to work with and what they would like to do. Some teachers have found it best to begin with a more structured setting where they assign the groups and tasks; as children learn to function independently, they are given more opportunity for decision making—selecting the task or the group to work with, or both. This kind of independence is, after all, the goal of cooperative learning.

Figures 4.3, 4.4, and 4.5 can be used as sign-up sheets for students. They can be used whether the teacher makes the assignments or the children decide themselves. It may be helpful for children to note on a form the activity they will participate in and the names of the members in their group (see Figure 4.3). Figure 4.3 can be used with children in late first grade and up. Figure 4.4 lets children

FIGURE 4-3 Group Activity Form

Date group formed_____

Activity selected_____

Circle how long you think the activity will take to complete.
1 day   3 days   1 week   1 ½ weeks   2 weeks

Members in the Group and Assigned Jobs

Leader_____

Recorder_____

Reporter_____

Other job assignments (list job and name):

_____

_____

_____

check off what they would like to do and it can be used at all grade levels. The teacher photocopies one sheet for each child to fill out at the beginning of literacy center time. Teachers with kindergartners and early first graders often use pictures along with words to depict activity choices. Figure 4.5 shows a sign-up sheet that can be used at different activity areas. Children sign the sheet when they select an activity or area in which to work, for instance, the author's spot, which is the writing area. At the author's spot a number is posted, such as 6, which means only six children can sign up for this area at a time. If six children are using it, others will have to find alternative activities such as quiet book reading, listening to stories on headsets, making a felt board story, and so on. For each of the activities there is a place to work, a sign-up sheet, and a number indicating how many students can participate at one time.

Roles Within Groups

Once groups are formed and activities decided on, the role of different individuals within the group needs to be decided. There must be a leader, who will outline the tasks to be accomplished and help delegate assignments (who will write the story, who will draw the pictures for the roll movie, etc.) so that everyone has a job. There also needs to be a recorder, who will write down the jobs to be done and which children are doing them. A reporter will share the accomplishments of

FIGURE 4-4   Check Activities to Do During Literacy Center Time

Name _____   Date _____

❑   1. Read a book, magazine, or newspaper.

❑   2. Read to a friend.

❑   3. Listen to someone read to you.

❑   4. Listen to a taped story and follow the words in the book.

❑   5. Use the felt board with a storybook and felt characters.

❑   6. Use the roll movie with its story book.

❑   7. Write a story.

❑   8. Draw a picture about a story you read.

❑   9. Make a book for a story you wrote.

❑ 10. Make a felt story for a book you read or a story you wrote.

❑ 11. Write a puppet show and perform it for friends.

❑ 12. Make a tape for a story you read or a story you wrote.

❑ 13. Record activities completed in logs.

❑ 14. Check out books to take home and read.

❑ 15. Use activity cards with directions for activities you do.

FIGURE 4-5   Author's Spot Sign-Up Sheet

Name	Date

the group. When working together, all the children must remember to take turns talking, stay on task, and be sure that everyone has a job related to the project.

Choosing Activities

To help children select activities, a list of possibilities is posted in the literacy center (see Figure 4.4). Activity cards, which list steps for carrying out individual literacy activities, help children organize their work. Figure 4.6 shows a sample activity card; others, representing projects of varying levels of difficulty, are provided in the resource section. Teachers of kindergarten and sometimes first grade make activity cards with drawings for beginning or emergent readers. Activity cards are printed on colored paper, laminated, and placed in a spot in the literacy center for children to select and use.

FIGURE 4-6   Sample Activity Card

Tell a Story Using the Felt Board

1. Select a leader for your group.
2. Select a book and the matching felt story characters.
3. Decide who will read and who will use the felt characters.
4. Take turns reading and placing the felt figures on the board.
5. Be ready to present the story to the class.
6. Record the activity in your log.
7. Check your work:

   How well was the story presented?

   How well did the group work together?

Children's choice of activities may often be determined by the materials and the space available. For example, they all can't choose to listen to taped stories if there are only five headsets. Teachers must devise systems to assure that there are appropriate numbers of children at different activities. This can be done by requiring each child to have an activity card for the material to be used, with the same number of activity cards printed as there are materials—for example, five activity cards for five headsets. When the activity cards are all taken, it means there is no more room for additional children.

> See the resource section for more activity cards (pp. 103–122).

Practicing Participation in Cooperative Settings

One of the purposes of literacy center time is for children to read and write collaboratively. Children need time to practice the different behaviors necessary to function in social settings. Initially, the children's goal in the literacy center should be learning how to cooperate, rather than to complete particular tasks. At first, some children may move from one activity to the next without completing any. As time passes, children will spend more time on projects, some of which may extend over several days or weeks. When literacy center time ends for the day and children haven't completed an activity, the project is stored for them to pick up later. Thus, teachers need to allow for storage space for unfinished activities.

Recording, Performing, and Evaluating Projects

When children work independent of their teacher they need to learn to select goals and to accomplish tasks. To provide encouragement, recording individual students' various accomplishments is a good idea. The groups will record their accomplishments; but it is also useful for individual children to keep records of what they have done. There are many different methods for doing this. Each student may have a collection of index cards on which are recorded his or her accomplishments (titles of books read, for example). The cards may be punched and hooked onto a ring that is hung on a bulletin board in the classroom, or stored in file boxes. Or students can maintain individual logs for recording completed tasks. Younger children and those who are in ESL classes and who do not know English well can be given logs with pictures for them to circle activities participated in.

> The resource section provides a log sheet form (pp. 104–105).

Children should also collect their original stories, poems, and other creations in individual manila folders or large envelopes. Just looking at what they have completed provides children with intrinsic rewards. These folders can also be shared with others in the class.

After completing a literacy center task, Adasha records it in her log.

The bulletin board displays rules on how to participate in literacy center time and index cards hung on rings for recording books read. Cards in the file boxes on the table record books checked out of the classroom library.

2. Guides or scaffolds literacy behaviors when help is needed.

3. Participates in activities with children at their request.

4. Observes activities and provides positive reinforcement for jobs well done.

To increase their supply of materials, teachers in different classes can share manipulatives and books. The children can also make materials for the literacy center, such as taped stories for the listening center and felt stories and roll movies for others to use. Their original stories can be bound and made part of the classroom library. Participating in these activities increases students' motivation, since they will feel an increased sense of ownership and respect for the area.

Sharing Completed Tasks

Children should share their accomplishments and can do so through a number of ways—book talks, demonstrations, reading what they've written, presenting an original puppet show, and so forth. Children evaluate their own projects, peers evaluate each other's, and teachers prepare evaluations as well. A few times a week, time is set aside for sharing accomplishments. The chance to show what they have done gives students an added reason for pursuing literacy activities.

The Role of the Teacher

In addition to preparing the environment and modeling literacy activities, the teacher has another very important task during literacy center time: interacting with the children. He or she:

1. Facilitates or initiates activities when children cannot get started alone.

Scheduling Social Literacy Activities

Teachers should model, or children engage in, pleasurable literature experiences every day. A special time can be set aside for children to be read to or for them to participate in other literature activities at a scheduled time daily. The activities can be embedded into other portions of the school day as well.

As mentioned earlier, children should have the opportunity to use the literacy center three to five times a week for thirty to forty-five minutes each time. Some teachers prefer to schedule longer periods three times a week, others prefer shorter periods five times a week. Literacy center time can be scheduled by itself, apart from other activities, but it can also be scheduled:

- As part of general center time, when other centers as well as the literacy center would be in use.

- As part of the reading-writing workshop when the teacher is not guiding an activity or presenting a lesson.

- As part of the reading group period or conference time. When the teacher is working with a small group of children or an individual child on skill development, the rest of the students can be involved in literacy center activities.

- As part of the language arts instructional block, which is often scheduled for an hour and a half in most elementary classrooms.

One of the most difficult tasks for teachers is to keep children engaged in activities while they work with groups or individual children to focus on skills. The teacher needs to give his or her full attention to the group or individual without being interrupted. The teacher can accomplish this by providing materials and guidance for students with differing ability levels to work independently in the literacy center.

Assessing the Collaborative Literacy Setting

Evaluating the success of the literacy center program should be carried out regularly. Teachers need to discuss with each other the physical design of their centers and how they could be improved. They need to share new ideas for using literature and learn from each other. They need to talk about issues concerning collaboration—for example, how to help children who are not on task, how to encourage different children to work together, how to help children try different tasks, and how to make sure that everyone has a leadership role at some time. Meeting provides teachers with a cooperative support system and an opportunity to learn from each other. In addition, it gives teachers the chance to experience firsthand what it feels like to participate in a cooperative setting, so that they can better understand how their children feel and the help they may need.

During periods when children engage in collaborative activities, teachers should observe the class to notice which students are on task, which ones need help getting started, and what activities the children choose. Centers can be changed to increase the productivity of the students. For example, teachers often move literacy centers from one area of the room to another, because they find a space that is bigger, brighter, or quieter. They add materials, such as books and manipulatives, to give children more choices. When necessary, changes can also be made in how literacy center time is managed.

Children's progress can be documented by recording anecdotes of activities, collecting writing samples, and audio- or videotaping groups at work and performances of completed activities. As mentioned earlier, children should be involved in self-evaluation. They can evaluate how they cooperated and the quality of their completed tasks. When finished projects are presented to the class, peers can offer constructive criticism. Children should be given the opportunity to make suggestions for improving the program and identify books and other materials they would like added to centers.

Parents and Literacy Center Time

Literacy center time provides a perfect opportunity for parents and other family members to become an integral part of the children's literacy program. All family members are welcome—parents, brothers, sisters, aunts, uncles, grandparents, and friends. Family members can come to watch, can participate as the children do, or can read to the class. They can share their cultural heritage by telling stories about the countries their families came from, or by reading stories from that culture. Children are proud to have family

 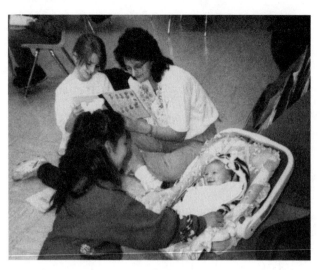

All family members are welcome at the literacy center—parents, brothers, sisters, grandparents, aunts, uncles, and friends. Eight-week-old Cody and his mother are visiting here.

members take part in school activities, and family members enjoy the time they spend in the center, while they learn about the workings of the literacy centers, a collaborative setting for learning and practicing reading and writing skills.

Scenes from the
Literacy Center

atrick had several copies of the story *Franklin in the Dark* (Bourgeois 1986), which he handed out to the other children. He also had a Big Book of the story. He asked his friends to sit in a circle and took the role of teacher. He began to read. After a while, he asked if anyone would like to have a turn, and Lisa volunteered. When Lisa had trouble with a word, Patrick helped her. Later Tiffany asked to be the teacher, and Patrick agreed to let her have a turn. When they had finished reading the story, Tiffany started a discussion about it. She asked if any of the children were afraid of the dark and if they would tell the group about something they were afraid of. A serious and enthusiastic conversation about what the children were afraid of then took place.

During literacy center time interactions such as the one described above happen frequently. Over the years, I have collected hundreds of hours' worth of field notes and videotapes of classrooms that used literacy center time and other collaborative strategies to motivate children's reading and writing.

Patrick had his friends sit in a circle and took the role of teacher. He began to read and asked the others if they'd like a turn.

My purpose was to see firsthand the nature of the activities that took place and their results. I also wanted to determine the processes involved in cooperative literacy activity that promoted independent reading and writing. In addition to the field notes and videotapes, interviews with teachers and children also helped me better understand the literacy activity that occurred during literacy center time (Morrow 1992; Sharkey 1992).

My classroom observations and videotapes revealed a variety of collaborative literacy behavior occurring during literacy center time, self-directed activities that involved children in decisions about what to do and how to carry through with their plans. Whether reading, writing, or using manipulatives, most activities were carried out in groups of two to five and involved both peer collaboration and peer tutoring. Overall, groups were friendly and mixed in gender, race, ethnicity, and ability, and included children with special needs. Children took charge of their own learning. They read orally and silently, they wrote, and they demonstrated literal, interpretive, and critical comprehension. The best way to describe the processes that occur during literacy center time, and to illustrate the different behaviors I observed in the classrooms, is to present anecdotes recorded during classroom visits.

Collaborative Activity During Literacy Center Time

How Groups Formed

With several decisions to make—to choose an activity, to work alone or with others and, if with others, with whom—children tended to observe groups before joining them. For example, Kim, Alexandria, and Tarene were reading joke and riddle books in a private spot sectioned off for reading. They snuggled together as they read. Damien stood nearby and watched for a short time, listening attentively as the jokes and riddles were read. Once he understood the nature of the group's activity, he asked to be included. The three allowed him to join them.

Some groups formed according to gender. At various times there were, for example, all-boy groups and all-girl groups, but overall, 41 percent of the groups I observed were mixed-gender groups. When groups did form by gender, their members frequently carried out activities that one could call sex stereotyped. The activity of mixed-gender groups was not sex stereotyped. Here are some examples (Morrow 1996, p. 60):

> Amber and Jessica searched the index of a cookbook and read the foods they liked. Jessica pointed to the phrase "chocolate chips" and said, "Look, Amber, on page 42 they have something with chocolate chips. Let's look at that." When they found the page, Amber said, "Wow, it's chocolate chip cookies. They're my favorite. Let's see how you make them."
>
> Matthew, Scott, and Andre worked on a roll movie for the story *Kick, Pass, and Run* (Kessler 1966). Matthew said, "Yo, you guys! Scott, you draw the football field, and Andre, you do the stands. I'll do the goal post."

> Mary, Tina, Jason, and Kevin were writing an original story and created felt figures to use on the felt board to present it to the class. When they finished, they decided to tape the story. The group designated Mary as the reader. Tina and Jason read silently as they followed along with her. Kevin followed the story and placed the felt characters on the felt board as they were mentioned. Tina and Jason made sound effects as needed for the story. After the taping, they played it back. They all listened and giggled.

As mentioned earlier, groups ranged in size from two to five; groups of two were the most common. Groups larger than five seemed to have trouble dealing with conflict. When groups had more then five, frequently one child would leave on his or her own. Girls tended to form groups of two most of the time, while all-boy and mixed groups were often larger. The number of children in self-selected groups suggests that when teachers form groups they should keep the maximum number at five.

Children formed groups, some according to gender. At various times there were all-boy and all-girl groups but, overall, the groups observed were of mixed gender.

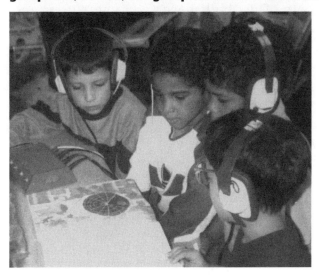

Although working cooperatively in groups was quite common, many children also chose to work alone. They usually read silently, but some did felt stories and chalk talks by themselves. Equal numbers of boys and girls chose to work alone.

Rules and Leadership Roles

Once formed, groups established their own rules and leadership roles. The rules involved decisions about the work that was to be accomplished, the responsibilities of the members for that work, and the quality of work that was acceptable. For example, Tesha and Cassandra decided to work together with a felt board story of *The Gingerbread Boy* (Galdone 1975a). The girls decided that they wanted to work on the floor. Cassandra told Tesha to carry the book and the felt characters and she would bring the felt board. Tesha said, "We need to work together to do this and we have to hurry in order to finish because we don't have much time." Cassandra said, "You read first and I'll put up the felt characters. When we are halfway through the story then I'll read and you put up the characters." The girls began the story, and halfway through, they switched roles. When they came to the rhyme "Run, run as fast as you can; you can't catch me, I'm the gingerbread man," they read together, laughing and saying how much fun they were having.

Within most groups, leaders emerged who were respected by other children. Ryan, Alex, and Gabe were working on the illustrations for a story they had written called "The Golden Sword." They spread out a large picture of a castle, and Ryan began to outline it in black marker.

Ryan: Alex, go get a black marker and help me outline this.

Gabe: Where should I start?

Ryan: Right over here. (*Alex returns with the marker.*) Alex, go get a red crayon.

Alex: Why, Ryan?

Ryan: Because we forgot to color this.

Alex: Will a red pencil do?

Ryan: I guess so. But Alex, we also need a blue crayon.

Alex: What do we need it for?

Ryan: We forgot to color in the water over here.

Gabe: What color should I do the sky?

Ryan: Blue will look good. (Morrow 1996, pp. 61-62)

Collaboration Within Groups

When groups formed, their members collaborated by helping each other, taking turns, sharing materials, and offering information. For example, Adasha and Tiffany decided to do a felt story together. Adasha said, "I want to do this one, *Cloudy with a Chance of Meatballs*" (Barrett 1978).

Tiffany said, "Let's do *Animals Should Definitely Not Wear Clothing*" (Barrett 1977).

"I know," said Adasha, "We'll do them both. They both have the same author and illustrator."

The girls decided to do *Cloudy with a Chance of Meatballs* first. Margaret and Tracey joined them, but sat quietly while Adasha moved the felt figures on the board and Tiffany read. After the story was finished, Margaret asked if she and Tracey could read. Everyone agreed, but decided that they would read the other book, *Animals Should Definitely Not Wear Clothing*. Margaret read and Tracey moved the felt figures while Adasha and Tiffany listened.

Peer Tutoring

Peer tutoring was frequent, with one child offering guidance and assistance to a peer who needed help. Children often whispered words and hints to help each other with words, spelling, or decisions about literacy projects. The help was often reciprocal: students would offer equal amounts of help to each other. They sought each other's opinions and offered positive reinforcement to each other. For example, Esther and Charo were reading a book of rhymes. Although both children also attended basic skills classes, in this situation Charo was able to take the typical teacher's role and help Esther with words she didn't know. Charo opened the book and selected a rhyme. Esther looked at the page and started to read, "'Old Mother . . .' What does that next word say?" Charo said, "That says 'Hubbard.' Now you read the rest." Esther continued, "'She went to the . . .' She paused and Charo helped again: "It says 'cupboard.' See, it rhymes with 'Hubbard.'" "Oh, yeah," said Esther, and she continued to read, "'to get her poor dog a bone.'"

Charo said, "Wait, Esther, we forgot. You gotta read it again, and this time start with the title of the poem first."

Conflicts

Although collaboration was more evident than conflict during group activities, conflicts did occur. Many involved selecting specific activities, sharing materials, and taking turns, and most were easily resolved. Other conflicts concerned specific questions within the activities themselves—deciding how to spell a word, identifying a word from the printed page, determining how to write a story cooperatively. Such conflicts were usually settled by discussion, by looking up words in a dictionary, or by seeking help from others. Learning theories suggest that learning occurs when conflict arises and those involved figure out how to settle it (Piaget and Inhelder 1969). The following episode demonstrates one such incident.

Zarah and Shakiera were writing a story together based on the movie *A Fish Called Wanda*. Zarah wrote the title, "A Fish Called Wander." Shakiera looked at it and said, "That's not the way you spell *Wanda*. It is W-A-N-D-A, not W-A-N-D-E-R." Zarah looked at her title and disagreed. "I'm right," she insisted. "I wrote a story about how I wander around my house and that is the way I spelled it, and it was right."

Children collaborate on projects and tutor each other as they work together writing stories by hand or on the computer.

Shakiera then said, "You've got the words mixed up. *Wanda* is a name, and *wander* is when you walk around, do you understand?" Reluctantly, Zarah agreed that Shakiera must be right, and she changed the spelling of the word.

Zarah continued writing while Shakiera dictated: "A fish called Wanda was a talking fish who had magic."

Zarah commented, "She had more than magic. She had magic powers."

"But that's what *magic* means," said Shakiera. "It means you have powers, so you don't have to say it."

"I think you do," said Zarah, "so that people really know how strong she was."

"I guess that's okay," said Shakiera. "You can write that she had magic powers."

Literacy Behavior

Students' collaborative behavior centered on literacy activities during literacy center time. The activities they engaged in were active and manipulative. They fell into four categories: oral reading, silent reading, writing, and use of manipulatives.

Oral Reading

Oral reading was a common practice during literacy center time. Oral reading provides practice with pronunciation, intonation, pacing, and performance. It also provides the teacher with evaluative information concerning reading proficiency. During literacy center time children read to each other aloud, in pairs, in small groups, and alone. They shared books, magazines, and newspapers. For example, Larry grabbed the book *The Magic School Bus Lost in the Solar System* (Cole 1990) from a bookshelf in the library corner. "I gotta read this book again," he said to Bryan. "It's neat."

The boys sat down on the carpet. Shon, who was standing close by, asked if he could read too and they agreed. Larry began reading, then Bryan took a turn and so did Shon. They listened attentively to each other. When they finished, the boys chose another book to read together (Morrow 1996, p. 64).

Children selected narrative stories to read as well as books associated with content areas they were studying. Mercedes and Patricia selected a book that was featured in their science unit on the changing earth: *Bringing the Rains to Kapiti Plain* (Aardema 1981). They decided to read it and use felt figures to illustrate the story. Patricia got the book, and Mercedes brought over the felt board and story characters. Patricia said she would read, and Mercedes agreed to place the figures on the board at the right time. Patricia read aloud, and Mercedes followed along in the book. When they finished reading, they discussed the story. They agreed that it was good that it finally rained because there was a drought in the jungle and all the animals were thirsty and would have died and all the plants were brown and dying.

In traditional classroom settings, the opportunity for oral reading is limited and often tedious for those who are made to listen. In the literacy center, children choose to read orally often and others may choose to listen or not, making the oral reading experience both productive and pleasant. Asking children to read orally in front of others can be unpleasant and threatening, yet during literacy center time children willingly participate in oral reading without being asked.

Silent Reading

Research has demonstrated a relationship between the amount of time spent reading and reading achievement (Anderson, Fielding, and Wilson 1988; Greaney and Hegarty 1987; Morrow 1990, Taylor, Frye, and Maruyama 1990). In the past, schools established periods of sustained silent reading. These periods tend to be somewhat contrived, since everyone is made to do the same thing at the same time. The literacy center approach gives children the opportunity to read silently, but it also allows them to decide whether they wish to read silently or engage in some other literacy activity.

Silent reading was apparent in many observations of literacy center time. Children read alone and sometimes together. They would curl up on a rug, leaning against pillows or each other, holding stuffed animals as they read. They read at their desks, in the closets, and under desks and tables. One child read silently while walking slowly around the classroom. One group I observed was typical: Jon was sitting in the rocking chair with Jenny, reading. Ben was leaning against a pillow reading the newspaper, and Jessy was leaning against him so he could read from the newspaper too. Doreen and Kelly were in the coat closet reading the same book together, and David was sprawled on the rug with *Space Rock* (Buller and Schade 1988).

In interviews both children and teachers said that the reading children were doing during literacy center time—including both oral and silent reading—was improving their ability as readers and writers, especially since they were doing so much of it. They also said that the help with reading that was readily available from the children's peers and their teacher during literacy center time made them better at reading.

Children also chose to do silent content area reading during their time in the literacy center. For example, one group of children decided to continue their study of plants, a unit in science they were concentrating on. As they were looking for books to read, Jovanna said, "Hey, you guys, I have an idea. Let's all read a book about plants." She went to the featured plant books, which were displayed because plants was the topic being studied in science, and distributed them to group members. "Who wants *Miss Harp in the Poison Ivy*

Case [Lexau 1983]?" Phillip took that one. Next she held up *A Tree Is Nice* (Udry 1956). Tyshell asked for that one. The next book was *Johnny Appleseed* (Moore 1964). Adasha raised her hand, and Jovanna gave that one to her. There were two left: *Discovering Trees* (Florian 1986) and *Cherries and Cherry Pits* (Williams 1986). Jovanna said, "Josh, I think you'll like *Discovering Trees,* and Kendra, you take *Cherries and Cherry Pits.*" They took their books, found a spot on the rug with a pillow or stuffed animal and began reading. When they finished, each took a turn telling about his or her story.

Writing

Initially literacy center time was simply to be a time for independent reading. But children either asked for writing materials or found them on their own and began writing. They used the materials in the literacy center writing as well as reading. They wrote new episodes for Harold in *Harold and the Purple Crayon* (Johnson 1955), a character featured in many stories. They wrote stories about the puppets and felt characters in the center. Their writing was based on their interest, experiences, current events, and even fiction they had read. Stories were written about news events, sports, and topics being studied in class, such as plants or dinosaurs. Children made up episodes for popular television shows. Others created computer games with illustrations and dialogue. Still others wrote biographies about popular rock stars with illustrations cut from magazines.

We know that during play at home, children write naturally about things that mean something to them (Gundlack et al. 1985; Holdaway 1979; Taylor 1983). Literacy center time provided a homelike environment in which writing could occur often and naturally.

Children wrote in pairs and small groups more often than alone, and their writing projects sometimes lasted for an entire period or longer. Such projects often became performances presented to the class in the form of puppet shows, roll movies, stories with musical background, plays with scenery, and so forth. The projects were self-sponsored and self-directed by the children. Here is an incident related to narrative writing: Paul and Kevin are writing together. Paul said, "I'm writing a series of stories. Each book is a different part but about the same character. I have *The Horse Named Jack, Jack Becomes a Police Horse,* and now I'm on the third called *Jack Enters a Horse Race.*" Kevin asked, "Can I read the one where he's a police horse?" Paul answered, "Okay, but you really should read *The Horse Named Jack* first since they go in order" (Morrow 1996).

As with reading, writing occurred all over the classroom. In one case, the table at the author's spot could fit only about three children, so students wrote sitting on the floor and at their desks. They often moved their desks together to make a large work surface at which they all could write together.

In interviews, teachers and children said that the children's writing was improving because they did so much of it. Teachers expressed surprise that children who would never write before were now choosing to do so. Teachers were also amazed at the variety of topics children wrote about. According to Graves (1975), when given the choice of what to write, children write more often and they write longer pieces.

As with reading, writing during literacy center time reflected content area teaching. The following was written by Kevin, a third grader, as a science story during literacy center time as a result of the teacher's integrating content subjects and literature and asking students to write science stories that included facts about science but that also used narrative plot structure.

My Dream About Space

I was set to go. I had trained for this for a long time. I had on my astronauts suit and the count down had begun 5, 4, 3, 2, 1, 0 blast off. My mission was to fly around the solar system and stop on as many planets and the moon as I could. I went flying through the air and along the way I saw several planets, there was Mars, Mercury, Jupiter, and Saturn. Saturn had many moons, it is yellowish with bands of different colors, like golden brown, and reddish brown. I almost got into a crash with an asteroid, but was lucky to miss it by a few inches. I decided to land on Mars first, to see what it was like. Wow was it hot. There wasn't any oxygen, thank goodness I had my tank along. Next we went to the moon. It is all sandy with craters. There aren't any trees, grass or leaves. Everything looks the same color. It was fun to jump up and down, I went so high because I didn't weigh much, it felt like I was flying. I had hoped to visit all nine planets on my trip through the solar system, but I was running out of fuel and decided it would be a good idea to go home. My space ride was exciting, I wanted to tell my mom about it. Suddenly I heard her calling. I felt like I was floating. I opened my eyes, I looked around, it was all a dream. My bed was my space ship and I had never left the ground.

Comprehension Development

Understanding what is read is the goal for proficient reading. Comprehension occurs at literal, inferential, and critical levels. Typically it is taught by posing questions for children to answer after they have read a passage. This activity is actually more of a test than a teaching approach. It does not involve the child actively in constructing meaning from text. During literacy center time, however, children were actively involved in constructing meaning, and they demonstrated comprehension at literal, inferential, and critical levels.

Literal comprehension requires the ability to remember and demonstrate an understand-

Children collaborated on writing projects during literacy center time and selected topics from their content area subjects such as dinosaurs, space, and the changing earth.

ing of the facts, sequence, and structural elements of a story. Christopher and Albert, for example, demonstrated this level of comprehension when they decided to retell *Amelia Bedelia's Family Album* (Parish 1988) using a roll movie. Chris told the story as Albert rolled the paper in the box to the appropriate scene. Chris retold the story using the dialogue from the book and including details of the story as he went along.

Inferential comprehension requires children to think beyond the text and involves understanding the characters' feelings, predicting outcomes, or putting oneself in the place of a character to determine another course of action—in other words, going beyond the simple facts and explicit statements of a story. For example, Darren decides to retell *Frog and Toad Are Friends* (Lobel 1970). He retold the story with puppets, changing

his voice and inflection as he interpreted the different characters.

Critical comprehension requires hypothesizing, analyzing, judging, and drawing conclusions. This level of thinking entails making comparisons and determining fact from opinion. Corey and Michael decided to listen to the taped story of *The Mitten* (Brett 1989) on the headsets. As they listened they read along, sharing a copy of the book. When they had finished listening to the story, Corey said, "You know, that story is a total fantasy. Does that author really expect us to believe that all of those animals fit into that little boy's mitten?" Michael said, "Well, you know, this is a folktale and lots of those have stuff in them that isn't true, except I think they want you to believe it is." Corey continued, "Well, maybe little kids would believe that this really happened, but I don't." Corey demonstrated critical comprehension in his discussion with Michael about whether or not the story of *The Mitten* could possibly be true.

In self-directed activities during literacy center time, children demonstrated their comprehension of the story in almost every incident recorded. None of these incidents involved the presence of a teacher or a lesson prepared by the teacher with questions for the children to respond to. Interview data revealed that children were aware that their comprehension was being enhanced during literacy center time. When asked "What do you learn during LCT?" half of the children responded that you learn to understand what you are reading and you learn a lot of new words. All the teachers mentioned that children were enhancing their comprehension, their sense of story structure, and their vocabulary development in the literacy center.

Appreciation for Reading and Writing

The ultimate goal of reading instruction is to develop the student into a person who has a positive attitude toward reading, appreciates and enjoys reading, and therefore will read. Children must associate reading with pleasure in order to read more and improve their reading ability. The fact that children engaged in literacy activities independently and in a self-directed manner was evidence of their positive attitudes toward literacy. There were few discipline problems during literacy center time, and few children were off task. The interview data consistently reflects positive attitudes. Children interviewed said such things as, "Reading and writing is fun. During this time it makes you happy, it makes you like to read and write because you can choose what you want to do and where you want to do it. You can get to decide if you want to read or write alone or with others. If you chose to work with others you can decide who you will work with." Teachers agreed with the chil-

dren; they said their students liked the element of choice—of activity, of place and space to work in, and with whom to work.

One episode in particular seems to encapsulate the pleasure children felt during literacy center time. Yassin was leaning on a pillow on the carpet reading a story. When he finished reading the book he sat up, raised the book over his head, and exclaimed out loud but to himself, "This is such a lovely story, it makes me feel so good, I think I'll read it again." He settled back down to his former position and began to read (Morrow 1996, p. 69).

Voluntary Participation by Children at All Skill Levels

The ability to participate voluntarily and in a cooperative fashion during literacy center time was a positive outcome for the children I observed. They enjoyed the literacy center a great deal, and they were able to stay on task. An important finding I made while working with the literacy center program over the years is the response of children who have difficulty learning. Many children with special needs were in classrooms where this program took place. A large percentage attended basic skills (Chapter 1) classes because their development in reading and writing was considered below grade-level performance. There were also children who attended ESL classes and children with social and emotional problems. All these children participated in literacy center activities as much as the children in the class without specifically designated certified learning problems. In fact, classroom observers often did not know which students fell into these groups until the teachers pointed them out. These children often emerged as leaders, and found activities in which they excelled and their special needs were often not obvious during this time.

All children were welcomed as group members. Individual differences did not seem to be an issue in the cooperative learning environment. For example, when Anita entered class in late fall, she spoke only Spanish. Unsurprisingly, she did not initially participate in literacy center activities. A few weeks later, however, she began to participate in activities, though always alone. One day, she selected a book from the literacy center and sat down on the rug to look at it. Lindsay sat down next to her and asked if Anita would like her to read the story to her. Lindsay understood Anita's smile to mean yes. She read, at the same time pointing to items in the illustrations and naming them for Anita, who after a while began to repeat the words. Lindsay seemed proud of herself in helping Anita, and Anita was proud of the fact that she was learning some English. But most of all, she was happy because she had found a friend. The two read together often during literacy center time.

Yassin was repeating second grade and receiving basic skills instruction. Yet he emerged as a leader during literacy center time, frequently organizing and carrying out projects with other children. One time he decided make a taped story. He stimulated the interest of James, Roseangela, Tamika, and Tara. He selected the story and delegated responsibility to those involved, deciding who would read which pages, when the group would choral-read certain parts, and where they would include musical background in their tape. With completion of the tape several days later, it was presented to the class and placed in the literacy center for further use.

Jonathan had been classified as an "elective mute": he never spoke. During literacy center time, he often sat on the rug and silently read books about sports. Other children sometimes sat next to him, looked on, and seemed to read from the same book with him. On several occasions, from recording on videotapes and reports by observers and his teacher, Jonathan was observed discussing the books with classmates around him—the only

Corine, a child in a classroom for the learning disabled, takes a lead role when reading a script for a puppet show that she wrote.

time anyone had seen or heard him speak during the entire school day.

During interviews, teachers commented that there seemed to be something for everyone in the literacy center. Children lacking in basic skills found literacy activities they could enjoy and succeed at. ESL children found ways to participate, and the literacy center appeared to be an excellent environment for enhancing language development. Children with emotional problems who tended to be withdrawn or disruptive became productive participants. Children with special needs did participate in conventional reading and writing activities, though reading and writing using manipulatives occurred more often and was a motivating factor for these children.

Parent Participation

Earlier I mentioned that parents should be invited to become an integral part of literacy center time. In the classrooms I have worked with, this involvement started off slowly and caught on with time. Parents came and brought younger siblings. They sat on the rug and read to small groups of children, or sat in the rocking chair and read to the entire group. Parents shared their special talents, hobbies, interests, and cultural background and tied them into what students were studying. In a unit on immigration to the United States, several parents who were immigrants themselves came to the literacy center to discuss their experience and share artifacts from their country. They proved to be a valuable resource, adding rich ideas to the classroom.

Teacher Participation

Traditional classroom arrangements often constrain the teacher as much as the student (Bossert 1979). In conventional recitation settings, teachers control how long a child may talk and on what subject, and students' opportunities to speak are limited (Sirotnik 1983). The teacher is also limited. Giving too much

attention to one student reduces instructional time for others and may also cause the group to lose focus.

During literacy center time, teachers could respond to the questions of one student or group without affecting the productivity of the others. In fact, the multitask structure of the literacy center, with its emphasis on collaborative learning, changed the teacher's role from information giver to "guide on the side." For example, as their teacher, Mrs. Pelovitz, circulated near where Sarah and Kim were writing a story, Kim asked Mrs. Pelovitz how to spell "suddenly." She spelled the word and then asked "Okay, suddenly what?" Mrs. Pelovitz then worked with Kim and Sarah to develop the story further. After Sarah read a portion of the story, Mrs. Pelovitz asked, "Since you talk about your sister making you mad, why not write about *why* she makes you mad?" Sarah said, "Okay, let's see, one thing is she just sits by the phone all day long waiting for it to ring for her and when it does, it is always her friends." Mrs. Pelovitz smiled and said to Sarah, "That would make me angry also."

The literacy center teacher acts as a participator and a facilitator, and offers positive reinforcement. For example, Mrs. Pelovitz sat

In a unit on immigration to the United States several immigrant parents came to the literacy center to discuss their experience and share artifacts from their country. Often their children translated what they had to say in their language to English. Children were proud when their parents visited the class.

down by Patrick, Lewis, James, Tiffany, and Shani to look at a roll movie they had just finished for *Mister Rabbit and the Lovely Present* (Zolotow 1962). She congratulated the group for a job well done. Mrs. Pelovitz then became the audience, as the students insisted on performing the roll story again for her. She commented at the end that the pictures were very vivid. James said he didn't know what "vivid" meant, so Mrs. Pelovitz defined the word for him. Before leaving the group she said, "If Maurice Sendak, the illustrator of this story, were to walk in the door of our room right now, he would think that he had drawn the pictures for the movie. Your work looks as good as his."

In the literacy center, teachers can respond to students' emerging insights (Golub 1988), and their literacy and social efforts are supported, rather than directed, by the teacher.

I noticed that, when teachers participated in literacy center time, they were generally relaxed because they did not feel the pressure of having to hold the attention of all the students at once. As a result, they were usually friendly and pleasant toward the students and generally more flexible than they were during recitation periods.

Teachers' Evaluation of Literacy Center Time

Teachers acted as facilitators, instructors, and participants during literacy center time. They helped children get organized, they gave instructional assistance when asked for, they participated with children and read their own books. They participated socially, interacting in a friendly manner with students. Teachers' interview comments were extremely consistent. They reported that at first they were concerned about the amount of time that the program would take away from other classroom activities, but that their feelings changed over time. By the end of the study, they saw lit-

eracy center time as an integral part of their reading instruction program. Teachers were also skeptical about getting children to work on tasks independently, but they were able to work through most of these problems with time. When asked what they learned from participating in the literacy center program it became apparent that they had changed some of their beliefs about literacy instruction and described changes in their behavior. Their responses to the question "What did you learn from participating in the literacy center program?" were revealing:

- The social, family atmosphere created by the literacy center was conducive to learning.

- Children are capable of cooperating and collaborating independently in reading and writing activities and learning from each other.

- In the atmosphere that provided choice of activity and with whom one worked, children of all ability levels chose to work together, a situation that did not normally occur.

- There was something for everyone in this program, advanced and slower children alike.

- It is the first time I realized that independent reading and writing periods are crucial for learning to read and write.

- It is the first time I realized how important it is for me to model reading and writing for children and interact with them during literacy center time.

- It made me more flexible and spontaneous and a facilitator of learning rather than always teaching.

- It taught me how to make reading and writing more appealing for children.

- I learned that the basal served to organize children's skill development, specifically in the area of word recognition. The literacy center program emphasized vocabulary and comprehension. Both programs complemented each other and should be used simultaneously.

- Children who don't readily participate in reading and writing did so during literacy center time. I think it is because they are the ones making the decisions about what they do.

Afterword

It is clear from the examples given in this book that creating literacy centers and giving students time for collaborative experiences that allow them to choose what they would like to do and with whom they would like to work motivates them to do a great deal of independent reading and writing. Certain factors contribute substantially to that positive effect, including:

- Appropriate physical design, furnishing, stocking, and use of classroom literacy centers.

- Modeled behavior by teachers in the form of pleasurable storybook reading and the use of literature manipulatives.

- Opportunities for children to use the resulting environment and select within it.

These factors provide the *context* that helps motivate the *process* of social interactive literacy activity that results in the *outcome* of increased literacy performance. Children are highly motivated in their desire to participate in collaborative literacy activities. Teachers reported that when they announced that literacy center time was to begin, children actually cheered. When the teacher would announce it was time to start cleaning up, that literacy center time was about to end, children would often object, saying they wanted just a few more minutes to finish a particular project or a book they were reading. This even happened when the next activity on the agenda was lunch or recess on the playground.

In addition to increased literacy activity and improved skills, children's positive attitudes toward reading and writing were evident from their enthusiasm as they participated in the literacy center time and from their comments in the interviews. Besides the element of choice, the manipulative nature of the materials was extremely important to the children. This promoted active involvement.

Students demonstrated their comprehension most often at the literal level, though inferential and critical comprehension was also evident. The children constructed meaning from text as they prepared plays and felt stories and discussed books as they read them together. They also frequently engaged in oral and silent reading, as well as writing. Children's appreciation for and interest in literacy activity was evident through their voluntary involvement, their enthusiasm, and their comments. Teachers commented that children participated voluntarily in activities they ordinarily might not be happy to be involved in when directed by the teacher.

Teachers and children consistently said that the element of choice and the large variety of literacy activities available played a very important role toward making literacy center time successful, even for children who had difficulty learning—for example, those with special needs. The literacy center environment worked very well for these students, both alone and in their dealings with other children. These youngsters are often isolates or discipline problems who have difficulty with typical classroom tasks, but during literacy center time children with special needs were able to become involved in literacy behavior that they enjoyed. They participated with other children or worked alone, and they were successful in the activities they chose to do. As one teacher said, "There seemed to be something for everyone. The literacy center time was successful since stigmas were removed, rewards were dispersed among all, and an intrinsic reward system was built into the program as children successfully completed tasks." Others have raised concerns as to the ability of such children to function in an environment where choices and responsibility for self-direction are given, rather than explicit instructions for proceeding with a task. My observations revealed that all children, regardless of their background or problems, were able to function in this setting.

During literacy center time, children made choices and self-directed their activity, but to enable them to function effectively, certain simple rules were established, as described in Chapter 4 on organization and management, such as (1) take only one material at a time, (2) replace materials to their exact spot before taking another, and (3) try to remain with one or two activities throughout the entire time. Since neither the children nor the teachers I worked with over the years were familiar with the literacy center approach at first, rules were reviewed prior to each period, and the teacher helped children with their choices when necessary. There were some problems with children's staying on task early in the program; however, within a month, with rules established, literacy behaviors modeled by teachers, and teachers acting as facilitators and participators, children were functioning well within this setting. Appropriate behavior appeared to depend on good classroom management organized by the teacher, rather than a child's educational level or cultural background.

As time went on most of the teachers I worked with, even those who were not comfortable with literacy center time initially, came to appreciate the importance of this type of setting for learning because of the results it brought about in the way of improved literacy achievement and more positive attitudes toward reading and writing. Many teachers began to see where this type of setting could fit in other parts of the school day; for example, during math, grouping was necessary for skill instruction, so teachers developed math centers with materials and the same kind of format as literacy centers for children to work on math in a collaborative manner. Teachers also began assigning collaborative activities for social studies and science that children could work on during literacy center time or some other time set aside for this type of setting. Collaborative learning that is independent of the teacher has many

benefits, and children should have ample opportunity to participate in such a setting for portions of the school day.

What occurred in the literacy centers reflects Holdaway's (1979) theory of developmental learning discussed earlier in the book, which is characterized by self-regulated, individualized activities and frequent social interaction with peers and adults in an environment rich with materials where whole acts of reading and writing can occur by choice. He defines four processes that enable children to acquire literacy abilities:

1. Observation of literacy behaviors, such as being read to or seeing adults and children engaged in reading and writing. During literacy center time children engaged in reading and writing and observed and emulated the behavior of both their teachers, who engaged in reading and writing with them, and of their peers, who were involved in these literacy activities as well.

2. Collaboration, which involves social interaction when engaging in literacy activity with peers or adults who provide motivation, encouragement, and guidance. During literacy center time children encouraged each other to participate, they tutored each other, and the teacher acted as a facilitator, providing help whenever it was needed.

3. Practice, which involves children trying out what they have learned by engaging in reading and writing either alone or with others. Children had plenty of opportunity to practice their learning during literacy center time.

4. Performance, which involves the child's sharing what has been learned and seeking approval from supportive, interested peers and adults. In other words, when a task is prepared for an audience, the reason for carrying it out becomes purposeful. Children demonstrated what they learned during lit-

eracy center time by discussing books read, reading their own stories to others, and performing stories using manipulatives such as puppets.

Literacy center time, although productive and important, does not take the place of more traditional types of literacy instruction. Without traditional strategies as well, instructional programs for reading and writing would be imbalanced and incomplete. The literacy centers described in this book focused on literature as the main source of activity. At the end of Chapter 2, I mentioned several other types of materials that are important for word analysis skill development and should be an important part of a literacy center.

A good way to characterize the success of the strategies discussed in this book is through the responses of teachers and children to interview questions that asked them to compare the components of the literacy center program to more traditional literacy programs (Morrow 1992).

On the question "What do your children like about the literacy center program?" teachers cited the following:

- Children like choices and self-directed activities, such as whether to read or write alone or with others and whether to use story manipulatives such as felt boards or taped stories alone or with others.

- Children also like teacher-directed literature activities, such as being read to by the teacher and the teacher's demonstrating creative storytelling such as chalk talks, roll movies, sound stories, and so forth.

- Children like the literacy center with its elements of comfort—the rocking chair, the rug, the pillows, and the stuffed animals.

To the question "What did the children learn from participating in the program?" responses were as follows:

- Children learned to participate voluntarily in literacy center time. They learned to cooperate when participating in literacy activities, and they were willing to help each other, engaging in peer tutoring.

- Children developed a positive attitude toward reading. They said they like to read, and they participated in literacy center time voluntarily and with enthusiasm.

- Children learned many literacy skills. Vocabulary and comprehension were enhanced; their sense of story structure was improved; the skills learned in traditional programs were reinforced; and their knowledge about authors and illustrators was increased.

Children were also asked various questions about the program (Morrow 1996). To the question "What do you like about the literacy center program?" they noted the following:

- The social atmosphere and choices in the program:
  "You can choose what you want to read, like reading long books, short books, hard books or easy books, roll stories, felt stories, and other stuff."
  "You can work with your friends on reading and writing, which makes it fun to do."
  "Kids who have problems that are left back and have to go to special classes can get help from their friends during literacy center time."
  "Teachers help you during literacy center time."

- Positive attitudes toward activities:
  "There are lots of good books that I like to read."
  "When you read during literacy center time it makes you feel happy."
  "Writing is fun in the author's spot with other kids."
  "The felt stories, tape stories, and other stuff are fun."

- Literacy activities they liked:
"I get to read a lot."
"I can write a lot."
"I tell felt stories, tape stories, and chalk talks."

- The literacy center environment:
"I like the Book Nook, it is cozy, it's a special place. You read on the carpet, in the rocking chair, and leaning on pillows."
"I would like the Book Nook to have more books."
"I would like to be able to use the Book Nook on more days."
"The only thing the Book Nook needs to make it better is some food, like a snack bar."

To the question "What do you learn in the literacy center program? children said:

- "You learn to read better because you read a lot."

- "You learn to understand what you are reading."

- "You learn a lot of new words."

- "You learn that authors and illustrators are real people just the same as you."

- "You learn how to read better because kids who read good help you during literacy center time."

To the question "Do teachers act the same during the literacy center program as they do in your regular reading program?" children responded:

- "In regular reading the teacher says you have to read this now. During literacy center time she lets you choose what you want to read or write."

- "The teacher reads to you and with you in the literacy center; she never does that in the regular reading time."

- "During regular reading the teacher makes you work; during literacy center time you read."

- "During regular reading, the teacher is bossy, talks to everyone at once, and doesn't help very much. During literacy center time she talks to everyone by themselves, helps us, and does stuff with us like a friend."

I have helped many teachers prepare their classrooms and organize and manage periods for collaborative literacy experiences and pleasurable literature activities that motivate children. I have received many letters from children in classes where teachers have implemented such strategies. I can think of no better way to conclude this book than by sharing some of these letters with you.

Dear Dr. Morrow,

Thank you for telling my teacher about literacy center time. It makes reading more fun than it really is. I always look forward to it every day. We don't get to have it every day, but I ask anyway.

From
Thomas Smith

Dear Dr. Morrow,

Thank you for giving us the idea for literacy centers and literacy center time. A lot of kids like it. I am doing a report on a story about *The Haunted Well* book, it is going to be a felt story. I am also helping my friend she is doing a stick puppet show on *Elizabeth Blackwell*. I have not done my characters yet but I am going to do them soon. Most of the time I help my friend and sometimes I work on my story.

From
Michelle Highland

Dear Dr. Morrow,

Thank you for teaching my teacher about literacy centers and literacy center time. It is very interesting and fun. Please tell these teachers how to do it too, Mrs. Riger, Mrs. Minor, and Mrs. Mitchille, they really need it in their classrooms. Do you have any more ideas like that for school? If you do, then please, please tell them to my teacher and the other ones I mentioned too. . . .

Sincerely,
Michael Toffey

Contents

PART

3

All About Books   185

PART
4

Becoming
Successful Writers   205

PART
5

Special Events   215

Part 1

Organization and Management of the Literacy Center

This section is meant to provide early childhood and elementary education teachers (K–6) with resources and suggestions for organizing and managing the classroom literacy center effectively. The lessons include specific ways to organize materials and manage literacy center time as well as how to encourage the use of the literacy center to promote students' voluntary reading and writing within school and at home. Each lesson motivates children to share their daily literacy experiences through such activities as book talks from the author's chair, story retellings using authentic props, and journal entries about favorite literacy activities.

Introduction to
Literacy Center Time

Purpose

- To introduce materials in the literacy center.
- To establish rules for literacy center time.

Materials

See "Suggested Literacy Center Materials" below.

Activity

 Bring children into the literacy center. Explain that they will have the opportunity to engage in daily literacy activities using the many books and materials available.

Introduce and demonstrate the variety of materials and activities for use during literacy center time. Explain that they can work alone or with others.

Go over the following rules with the class:

- Handle materials carefully.
- Select only one or two items at a time.

- Put completed books away before selecting another.
- Treat each other with respect.

Allow students to explore the materials. If necessary, assist children in using materials. Be prepared to closely supervise literacy center time during the first several days. When the class has mastered using the materials independent of the teacher, begin to model positive reading behavior by practicing silent reading or participating in students' literacy activities.

Suggested Literacy Center Materials

When designing the literacy center, keep in mind that it should be a comfortable place where students with a variety of different interests and abilities can gather to engage in literacy activities. The following suggested materials have been proven to intrinsically motivate children toward reading and writing.

To Create the Environment:

open-faced bookshelves

posters that advertise reading and writing and increase the imagination

rug

pillows

rocking chair

table and chairs

quiet place for reading (beneath a counter, a box, etc.)

"Library Corner" and "Literacy Center" signs

mural paper hung on wall for impromptu writing

bookshelf labeled "Literacy Center Books Only"

bookshelf labeled "Books That Can Go Home"

Materials for Activities:

approximately 100 books

literature-based videos, television, and VCR

library book checkin/checkout system (see Lesson 2)

tape recorder

headsets and audiotaped stories

audiotapes of musical stories

puppets

stuffed animals and props that are associated with books

felt board with figures to accompany various books

materials for children to create their own felt board figures: felt strips, construction paper, markers, scissors, glue

materials for children to write, illustrate, and publish their own books: construction paper, writing paper, stapler, pencils, crayons, scissors, glue

roll movie box and materials for making roll movies: shelving paper, pencils, crayons

popsicle stick figures to accompany various books

materials for children to make popsicle stick figures: popsicle sticks, construction paper, scissors, markers, glue

2
Checking Books out of the Classroom Library

Purpose

- To establish a checkout system for books in the classroom library.
- To encourage daily reading.

Materials

Index Card Option:

two different color 5-by-8-inch index card file boxes (one labeled "Books Out" and the other "Books In")

colored index cards (two per child, one for each box)

white index cards

Log Option:

loose-leaf binder, clipboard, or spiral notebook with separate page for each child, each page with "Date Out" and "Date In" columns.

Both Options:

stickers used as rewards for book returns

bookshelf of books marked "Take-Home Books"

Activity

Show the bookshelf marked "Take-Home Books." Explain that books can be checked out of the classroom library to be read at home.

Show the two index card boxes or the log. Explain the procedure for checking books out.

If using the file card system, children take a blank index card from the "Books Out" box, write their name, the title of the book they are borrowing, and the date. Then they put the card behind the colored index card that has their name on it in the "Books Out" box. When the book is returned, they remove the index card from the "Books Out" box, write the date returned, and place it in the "Books In" box behind the colored index card with their name on it. (The sample provided on page 101 has headings for each entry.)

If using the log, students have their own page in a loose-leaf binder or spiral notebook. When checking out a book, they write their name, the title of the book, and the date in the "Date Out" column. When the book is returned, the date is written in the "Date In" column (see sample on page 100).

Book Checkout Form for Loose-Leaf Binder or Clipboard

Name:

Title of Book	Date Out	Date In

Sample Index Card

Your Name	Book Title	Date Out	Date In

3

Keeping a Record of Books Read

Purpose

To motivate voluntary reading by keeping track of books read.

Materials

3-by-5-inch index cards

one index card box, plastic bag, or spiral notebook per child

markers

Activity

Let children know that they should keep track of books they read throughout the school year.

Once a child finishes a book, encourage him or her to write the book's title and the date completed in a notebook or log or on an index card.

Tell children to write about and illustrate their favorite part of the story or favorite character(s). If using the index cards, children should place them in the box or plastic bag when completed.

The teacher should review students' logs or cards weekly or at least every other week. This system can serve as an authentic assessment of literacy development.

4

Using Activity Cards

Purpose

To help children organize themselves to accomplish goals in social collaborative groups (see Chapter 4).

Materials

an activity card, for instance, "Use a Felt Story"

accompanying materials, for instance, a felt board and story characters

accompanying book

Activity

Activity cards that have already been introduced by the teacher are available to the children. (See samples on pages 106–122.)

The teacher may choose to organize groups of children and assign an activity card for them.

The teacher may choose to organize groups of children and allow them to select an activity card for the group.

The teacher can display four or five activity cards to choose from and ask the children to decide what they would like to do.

When groups and activities are selected, children go to the designated area in the classroom to carry out the task.

The children follow the steps outlined on the activity card by assigning tasks to everyone in the group and carrying out the activity.

When the activity is complete, the children fill out log forms. The sample on page 104 is for younger children who are not yet able to write, and they circle the activity they have completed. Those who are able to write fill in a log form like the sample on page 105.

Photocopy activity cards onto colored paper, laminate, and place in a convenient spot for children to select and use.

Sample Log Form for Younger Children

Name:

Date:

Activity:

Read by myself	Read to a friend	Roll movie	Taped story	Felt story	Write a story	Make a felt story, roll movie, or picture	Other

Date:

Activity:

Read by myself	Read to a friend	Roll movie	Taped story	Felt story	Write a story	Make a felt story, roll movie, or picture	Other

Sample Log Form for Older Children

	Read by myself	Read to a friend	Roll movie	Taped story	Felt story	Write a story	Make a felt story, roll movie, or picture	Other
Name:								
Date:	**The activity that I worked on today was:**							

Use a Felt Story

1. Choose a felt story to use.

2. Get the book, felt board, and characters.

3. Read the book and practice telling the story with the felt pictures.

4. Be ready to tell the story to the class at sharing time.

5. Record your activity in your literacy log.

6. Check your work:
   How well was your project done?
   How well did you work as a group?

Make a Felt Story

1. Choose a book to make into a felt story, or write your own story for a felt story.

2. If this is your own story, begin by writing the story. Decide which characters and what other things will be in the felt story.

3. If this is from a book, read the book and look carefully at the pictures. Decide which characters and what other things will be in your felt story.

4. Get the things you'll need: paper, drawing and coloring materials, glue, felt.

5. Be sure everyone has a job: writer, drawer, colorer, gluer, storyteller.

6. Draw the pictures you want to have in the story. Glue felt on the back of them.

7. When you are done, practice telling the story with the felt pictures.

8. Be ready to tell the story to the class at sharing time.

9. Record your activity in your literacy log.

10. Check your work:
How well was your project done?
How well did you work as a group?

Use a Prop Story

1. Get the props and the book that goes with them.

2. Read the story.

3. Retell the story using the props. Be sure everyone has a job. Take turns telling the story and holding the props.

4. Try new things:
   Tell your own story with the props.
   Make new props to add to this story.
   Make new props for a story you wrote.

5. Be ready to tell the prop story to the class at sharing time.

6. Record your activity in your literacy log.

7. Check your work:
   How well was your project done?
   How well did you work as a group?

Use Puppets

1. Choose the puppets you'd like to use.

2. Choose a book for the puppet story, or write your own story for the puppet story.

3. If this is your own story, begin by writing the story. Decide which characters will be in the puppet story and what they will do and say.

4. If this is from a book, read the book. Decide which characters will be in your puppet story and what they will do and say.

5. Tell the story using the puppets. Take turns using the puppets and telling the story.

6. Be ready to tell the story to the class at sharing time.

7. Record your activity in your literacy log.

8. Check your work:
   How well was your project done?
   How well did you work as a group?

Make a Puppet Story

1. Choose a story to make into a puppet show, or write your own story for a puppet show.

2. If this is your own story, begin by writing the story. Decide which characters will be in the puppet story and what they will do and say.

3. If this is from a book, read the book. Decide which characters will be in your puppet story and what they will do and say.

4. Get the things you'll need: paper, drawing and coloring materials, glue, sticks, etc.

5. Be sure everyone has a job: writer, drawer, colorer, gluer, storyteller, puppeteers.

6. Make the puppets for the story.

7. When you are done, practice telling the story with the puppets.

8. Be ready to tell the story to the class at sharing time.

9. Record your activity in your literacy log.

10. Check your work:
    How well was your project done?
    How well did you work as a group?

Use a Chalk Talk

1. Choose a book for the chalk talk.

2. Get the book and the materials you'll need: paper, markers or chalk, etc.

3. Read the book and look carefully at the pictures. Decide which parts of the story will be in your chalk talk.

4. Tell the story while you draw the pictures on the chalkboard or paper. Take turns drawing and telling or reading.

5. Be ready to tell the story to the class at sharing time.

6. Record your activity in your literacy log.

7. Check your work:
   How well was your project done?
   How well did you work as a group?

Make a Chalk Talk

1. Choose a book to make into a chalk talk, or write your own story for a chalk talk.

2. If this is your own story, begin by writing the story. Decide which parts of the story will be in the chalk talk.

3. If this is from a book, read the book and look carefully at the pictures. Decide which parts of the story will be in your chalk talk.

4. Get the things you'll need: paper, drawing materials, chalk.

5. Be sure everyone has a job: planner, drawer, storyteller, materials maker.

6. Draw the pictures you want to have in the story. Make any other materials you'll use.

7. When you are done, practice telling the story on the chalkboard.

8. Be ready to tell the story to the class at sharing time.

9. Record your activity in your literacy log.

10. Check your work:
    How well was your project done?
    How well did you work as a group?

Listen to a Taped Story

1. Choose a taped story to listen to with a friend or by yourself.

2. Get the things you'll need: paper, writing and drawing materials, storybook, tape recorder, tape.

3. Listen to the story and follow along in the book.

4. After the story, draw a picture of your favorite part.

5. Decide how you would change this story to have a different ending. If you are working with friends, decide on one idea together that you will write down. Take turns writing and sharing ideas.

6. Be ready to tell your ideas to the class at sharing time.

7. Record your activity in your literacy log.

8. Check your work:
   How well was your project done?
   How well did you work alone or as a group?

Use a Roll Movie

1. Get the things you'll need: roll movie box and book.

2. Read the book and tell the story with the roll movie. Take turns reading, telling, and turning the roll movie.

3. Be ready to tell the story to the class at sharing time.

4. Record your activity in your literacy log.

5. Check your work:
   How well was your project done?
   How well did you work as a group?

Make a Roll Movie

1. Choose a story to make into a roll movie, or write your own story for a roll movie.

2. If this is your own story, begin by writing the story. Decide which parts of the story will be in your roll movie.

3. If this is from a book, read the story and look carefully at the pictures. Decide which parts will be in your roll movie.

4. Get the things you'll need: paper, drawing and coloring materials, roll movie box.

5. Be sure everyone has a job: writer, illustrator, storyteller, reader, roll movie turner.

6. Make the pictures for your story on the roll paper. Put the paper into the roll movie box. Tape the ends of the paper onto the dowel.

7. When you are done, practice telling the story with the roll movie.

8. Be ready to tell the story to the class at sharing time.

9. Record your activity in your literacy log.

10. Check your work:
    How well was your project done?
    How well did you work as a group?

Quiet Reading

1. Choose something to read: a book, a magazine, a newspaper, etc.

2. Read alone or read with a friend.

3. Try some ideas:
   Take turns reading.
   Read to a friend.
   Listen to a friend read.
   Retell your story to a friend.
   Read the same book as your friend.
   Tell your friend about what you read.

4. Record your activity in your literacy log.

5. Check your work:
   How well did I read?
   How well did I understand?

Partner Reading

1. Choose a book to read.

2. Take turns reading the book. One person can read one page, then the next person reads the next page.

3. When you're done reading, take turns retelling the story to each other or to a stuffed animal.

4. Be ready to tell the class about the book at sharing time.

5. Record your activity in your literacy log.

6. Check your work:
   How well did you read and understand?
   How well did you work together?

What Will Happen Next?

1. Choose a book to read you haven't heard or read before.

2. Take turns reading the first few pages.

3. Stop reading and talk about what you think will happen next. Take turns talking.

4. Write your ideas down on paper.

5. Finish reading the book, taking turns.

6. At the end of the book talk about what you thought would happen and what really happened. Which way do you like the story better?

7. Tell the class about the story during sharing time.

8. Record your activity in your literacy log.

9. Check your work:
   How well did you read and write?
   How well did you work as a group?

118

Favorite Character Book

1. Look through the classroom library and choose a favorite character from one of the books. Here are some ideas, or you can choose your own:

   Clifford

   Frog and Toad

   Miss Nelson

   Miss Frizzle and
   the Magic School Bus

   Berenstain Bears

   Harold

   Curious George

2. Read the book you've picked out. Plan a new story with this character. Think about: Who else is in the new story? Where and when does the new story take place? What is the problem the main character has? What will happen to the characters? How will the problem be solved? How will the new story end?

3. Write the words to your story and make pictures for your book. Make a title page with the name of the book and the name of the authors and illustrators (you!).

4. Be sure everyone has a job. Take turns telling the story, writing the words, and making the pictures.

5. When you are done, staple your pictures together to make a book. Show the class your book during sharing time, then put it in the literacy center for others to read.

6. Record your activity in your literacy log.

7. Check your work:
   How well did you do the project?
   How well did you work as a group?

Journal Writing

1. Get the materials you'll need: journal, pencil, crayons.

2. Think about what you'd like to write about.

3. Write in your journal. Add pictures if you want to.

4. Record your activity in your literacy log.

5. Check your work:
   How well did you think of ideas?
   How well did you write?

Create an Original Book

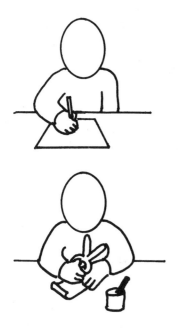

1. Decide on an idea for a book that the group will write.

2. Plan the story:
   Who is in it?
   Where and when does the story take place?
   What is the problem the main character has?
   What will happen to the characters?
   How will the problem be solved?
   How will the story end?

3. Write the words to your story and make pictures for your book. Make a title page with the name of the book and the name of the authors and illustrators (you!).

4. Be sure everyone has a job. Take turns telling the story, writing the words, and making the pictures.

5. When you are done, staple your pictures together to make a book. Show the class your book during sharing time, then put it in the literacy center for others to read.

6. Record your activity in your literacy log.

7. Check your work:
   How well was your project done?
   How well did you work as a group?

5

Sharing Completed Tasks

Purpose

To provide closure to daily literacy center activities.

Materials

Determined by the materials used during the day's literacy activities.

Activity

Create an environment where students feel comfortable sharing their enthusiasm and concern about the reading program.

Encourage children to share their thoughts and feelings, as well as their literacy accomplishments, with the class. An excellent forum for this is through the author's chair. The author's chair, usually located in the literacy center, is a place where students can sit and share their favorite stories or read their original published books.

Time should be set aside to review the day's activities as well as to remind children of materials needed for the following day (e.g., props, returned books).

Close the day's program by reciting as a class the rhyme "Before you go to sleep tonight, read a book, then turn off the light."

A form for making bookmarks with this rhyme is provided on page 124. Photocopy on colored paper, color, cut, and laminate.

Bookmarks for Children

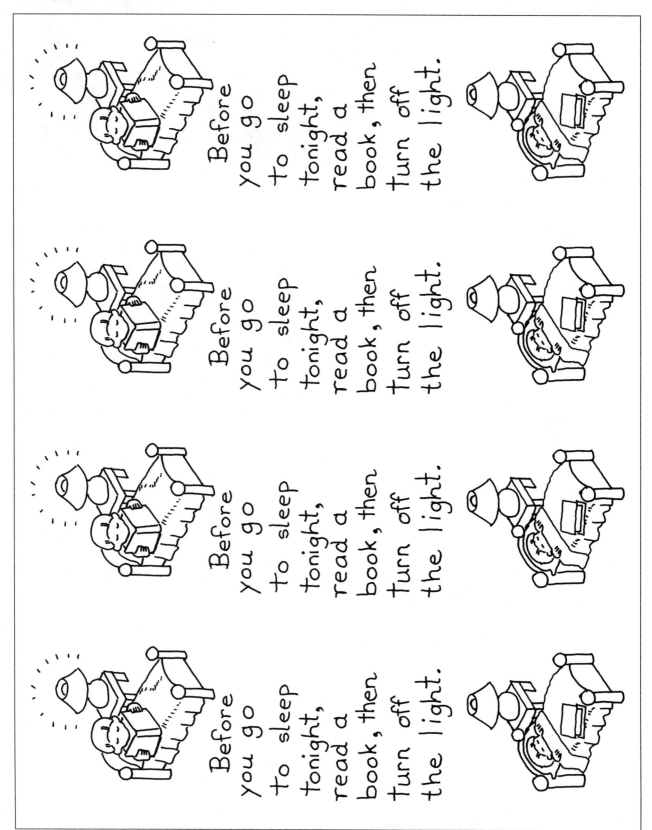

Part 2

Storytelling Techniques

This section is meant to provide teachers with creative storytelling techniques appropriate for kindergarten through sixth-grade levels. All the activities encourage students to engage in enjoyable, independent, and collaborative projects that develop literacy and promote participation in reading and writing.

In each lesson a sample story is given to assist the teacher in becoming familiar with each storytelling technique. The stories are labeled as being suitable for grades K–2 (or K–3) or grades 3–6. However, all the activities can be used at any grade level by substituting a more appropriate story. Suggestions for additional books for grades K–2 and grades 3–6 are provided at the end of each lesson. When using chapter books in activities, as children in grades 3–6 are likely to do, they should choose a portion of the book—the introduction, a favorite scene or chapter—or do a plot summary as the basis of the activity.

A general strategy for all activities is to have the teacher model the storytelling technique and then have students retell the teacher's story and apply this technique to retell a favorite story, and to write, illustrate, and share their own story. Comprehension and word recognition skills have been embedded throughout the activities to aid the teacher in integrating skills instruction with a literature-based approach.

Felt Board Story

"A Bunny Called Nat" (grades K–2)

Purpose

To have students:

- Retell the teacher's sample story.

- Identify colors of characters depicted in the sample story.

- Create a felt board story using the characters and plot of a favorite book.

- Write, create, and present an original felt board story.

Materials

felt board

felt board characters: five bunnies, one each in gray, blue, yellow, green, and orange

See the following pages for instructions on making a multipurpose felt board and a template for the rabbit characters.

Activity

Introduce children to the felt board and demonstrate how characters stick to the board.

Tell the story while placing figures on the board at appropriate times. Ask students to recognize and identify the colors of the characters in the story.

Have children work with a partner to retell the sample story.

Have students choose a favorite book, create appropriate felt board characters, and present the story.

Have children write original stories and create felt board characters to be used in their retelling.

Sample Story: "A Bunny Called Nat"

(adapted from an anonymous tale)

Once upon a time there was a little gray rabbit and his name was Nat. One day he looked around and saw that all his brothers and sisters, cousins and friends were gray, too. He thought he would like to be different from them. So he said:

(Chorus:)   I'm a bunny called Nat,
            I'm funny and fat,
            And I can change my color
            Just like that (*snap your fingers*).

And suddenly Nat was a blue bunny. He was blue like the sky and blue like the sea. He was blue like the twilight and blue like the dawn. It felt nice and cool to be blue. He decided to take a look at himself in the pond. He hurried to the edge and admired his reflection in the water. He leaned over so far that SPLASH! He fell into the pond. Nat fell deep into the blue water and he couldn't swim. He was frightened. He called for help. His friends heard him, but when they came to the pond they couldn't see him because he was blue like the water. Fortunately a turtle swam by and helped Nat get safely to shore. Nat thanked the turtle. He decided that he didn't like being blue. So he said: (Chorus)

And this time, what color did he change himself to? Yes, he was yellow—yellow like the sun, yellow like a daffodil, yellow like a canary. Yellow seemed like such a happy color to be. He was very proud of his new color, and he decided to take a walk through the jungle. Who do you think he met in the jungle? He met his cousins the lion and the tiger. The lion and the tiger looked at Nat's yellow fur and said, "What are you doing in that yellow coat? We are the only animals in this jungle that are supposed to be yellow." And they growled so fiercely that Nat the bunny was frightened and he ran all the way home. He said: (Chorus)

And this time, what did he change his color to? Yes, he was green. He was green like the grass and green like the leaves of the trees. He was green like a grasshopper and green like the meadow. As a green bunny, Nat thought he'd be the envy of all the other bunnies. He wanted to play with his other bunny friends in the meadow. But because he was the color of the grass in the meadow, he could not be seen, and his friends just ran and jumped about him not seeing him at all or mistaking him for a grasshopper. So Nat the bunny had no one to play with while he was green. Being green wasn't much fun. So he said: (Chorus)

And what color was he then? Right, he was orange. He was orange like a carrot, orange like a sunset, orange like a pumpkin—he was the brightest color of all. He decided he would go out and play with all his brothers and sisters and friends. But what do you suppose happened? When his friends saw him, they all stopped playing and started to laugh, "Ha, ha, whoever heard of an orange bunny?" No one wanted to play with him. Nat didn't want to be orange anymore. He didn't want to be a blue bunny because if he fell into the pond no one could see him to save him. He didn't want to be a yellow bunny and be frightened by the lion and the tiger. He didn't want to be a green bunny because then he was just like the meadow and none of his friends could see him. And so he said: (Chorus).

Do you know what color Nat the bunny changed himself into this time? Yes, you're right. He changed himself back to gray. And now that he was gray all of his friends played with him. No one growled or laughed at him. He was gray like a rain cloud, gray like an elephant, gray like pussy willows. It felt warm and comfortable being gray. From that time on, Nat the bunny was always happy being a gray bunny, and he decided that it's really best being just what you are.

Books Appropriate for Felt Board Stories for Grades K–2

Cherry, Lynne. *The Great Kapok Tree*. New York: Harcourt Brace, 1990. A hunter falls asleep in the rain forest and is visited by the creatures who live there. Together they convince him not to cut down the great kapok tree. Felt board figures: kapok tree, man, boa constrictor, bee, monkey, toucan, macaw, cock-of-the-rock, tree frog, jaguar, porcupine, anteater, three-toed sloth, child.

Demi. *The Artist and the Architect*. New York: Holt, 1991. Chinese folktale about a rivalry between an artist and an architect. Felt board figures: emperor, architect, artist, parchment, castle, house connected by tunnel, smoke.

Kipling, Rudyard. *How the Camel Got Its Hump*. New York: Macmillan, 1994. Classic fable about the consequences of laziness. Felt board figures: camel with no hump, camel with hump, genie, horse, ox, dog.

Books Appropriate for Felt Board Stories for Grades 3–6

Choose the introduction or a favorite scene or chapter, or do a plot summary. Some main characters have been listed.

Atwater, Richard, and Florence Atwater. *Mr. Popper's Penguins*. New York: Dell, 1978. Mr. Popper, a house painter, adds twelve penguins to his family. He gets larger food bills, some messy situations, and a lot of laughs. Felt board figures: man, woman, girl, boy, twelve penguins.

Blume, Judy. *Freckle Juice*. New York: Macmillan, 1971. Andrew Marcus is obsessed with Nicky Lane's freckles and gets caught counting them in school. Sharon explains that the more juice Andrew drinks, the more freckles he can get. Felt board figures: boy without freckles, boy with freckles, girl, glass of juice.

Dahl, Roald. *James and the Giant Peach*. New York: Puffin, 1988. James, an orphaned boy, is sent to live with his mean and terrible aunts. But James is able to escape into a giant peach filled with funny characters. Felt board figures: boy, peach tree, one giant peach, skinny woman, heavy woman, grasshopper, ladybug, centipede.

Making a Felt Board

This board can be used as a felt board, as a Big Book stand, and for stick puppet shows (scenery can be made on the felt and the puppets held from the back top of the board).

Directions:
1. Lay the piece of corrugated cardboard flat. Pre-bend all flaps.
2. Set up front panel (see sketch). Line up A slots with matching B slots on bottom panel.
3. Insert tabs C from last panel through both A and B slots.
4. Pull through and lock into D slots. Your easel is set up.
5. Cover front of board with felt.

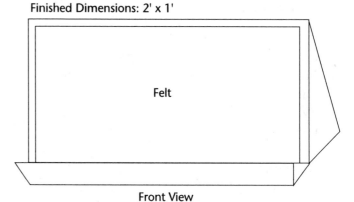

Finished Dimensions: 2' x 1'

Front View

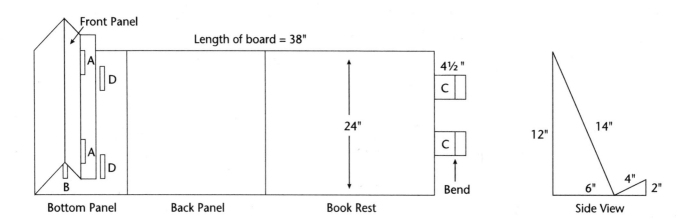

A Bunny Called Nat

Directions:
Use this template to make felt board characters. Make five bunnies: one for each color discussed in the story.

2

Prop Story

"The Chocolate Touch" (grades 3–6)

Purpose

To have students:

- Retell the teacher's sample story and concentrate on details in the retelling.

- Criticize and evaluate materials in choosing props for retelling a favorite story.

- Write and present an original prop story.

Materials

yellow pencil

brown pencil

silver coin

coin painted brown

red apple

apple painted brown

white glove

brown glove

Activity

Tell a story using props. Ask students to listen carefully for the important parts or the details of the story that make it a good story (without them the story would not be as interesting or make sense). Explain that these details help you choose what props to use in the retelling.

Have students retell the teacher's sample story using the props in correct sequence.

Have students choose props to retell a favorite story.

Have students write and present an original prop story.

Sample Story: *The Chocolate Touch*

by Patrick Skene Catling (New York: William Morrow, 1979)

Summary of favorite scenes:

John Midas loved chocolate. One day he found a mysterious old coin and used it to buy a box of chocolate from a strange candy store. John was upset to see that there was not a lot of chocolate in the box. But after he ate it, he found that everything he ate turned into chocolate.

John always chewed on his gloves (*show white glove*). His mother told him not to, but John didn't listen. Except this time something was different. Something tasted weird. His glove did not have the familiar leathery taste. He pulled his thumb out of his mouth and saw that the glove had turned into chocolate (*show brown glove*). John was so excited that he chewed and chewed until he ate the whole glove.

John's friend Susan was overjoyed about her birthday present. She ran to John to show him her new silver dollar (*show silver coin*). John had forgotten the strange things that had been happening and asked Susan if he could see if it was real silver. She replied yes, thinking that John was being silly, but challenged him to bite it. When John bit Susan's silver dollar, it too turned to chocolate in his mouth (*show brown coin*). John could not believe what was happening.

During school, John put a pencil in his mouth (*show yellow pencil*). When he pulled it out he was shocked. Not only did the part his mouth touched turn to chocolate, but the rest of the pencil did as well (*show brown pencil*).

When Susan and John went bobbing for apples (*show red apple*), they put their faces into the bucket. The water turned a muddy brown (*show brown apple*). Susan and John pulled their heads out of the water and found they were drenched in chocolate syrup. Now everything John touched turned to chocolate. It was getting frustrating.

Books Appropriate for Prop Stories for Grades K–2

Bond, Michael. *Paddington Bear*. New York: HarperCollins, 1960. A small bear found at Paddington Station becomes a family member. Props: stuffed bear with hat and coat, man, woman, girl, boy.

James, Simon. *Dear Mr. Blueberry*. New York: Macmillan, 1991. During summer vacation, Emily writes to her teacher, Mr. Blueberry, about a whale who ends up in the pond in her backyard. Props: girl, man, blue whale, envelopes, mailbox.

Rockwell, Thomas. *How to Eat Fried Worms*. Santa Barbara, CA: ABC-Clio, 1987. Two boys compete to prove that worms can make delicious meals. Props: frying pan, gummy worms.

Books Appropriate for Prop Stories for Grades 3–6

Fox, Mem. *Wilfrid Gordon MacDonald Partridge*. New York: Kane Miller, 1985. A boy helps an elderly friend rediscover her memories by sharing things that are meaningful to him. Props: egg, shell, medal, puppet, football, basket.

Howard, Elizabeth Fitzgerald. *Aunt Flossie's Hats (and Crab Cakes Later)*. New York: Clarion Books, 1991.   Sara and Susan share tea, cookies, crab cakes, and stories about hats when they visit their favorite relative, Aunt Flossie. Props: hats of various styles as described in book.

Zolotow, Charlotte. *Mr. Rabbit and the Lovely Present*. New York: Harper and Row, 1962.   A girl asks Mr. Rabbit to help her choose a birthday present for her mother. Props: apples, bananas, pears, purple grapes, and a basket to put them in.

3

Puppet Story

"I Know an Old Lady Who Swallowed a Fly" (grades K–2)

Purpose

To have students:

- Retell the teacher's sample story in order to recall the sequence of characters and events using puppets.

- Retell a favorite story using child-created puppets.

- Write and present an original puppet story.

Materials

Puppets may be of various types: hand, stick, finger, and face puppets. Face puppets are large enough for the children to stand in back of them and show their faces through the cutout portion. For the sample puppet story use a cutout of the old lady (see template on page 138). Create a clear plastic pocket for her stomach so each of the animals she swallows can be seen. Also needed are cutout figures of a fly, a spider (with string attached), a bird, a cat, a dog, a cow, and a horse (templates for each are provided on pages 139–140).

Activity

Tell the story and, as the old lady swallows each animal, drop it into her stomach. (The spider can be made to wiggle by using the string attached to it.)

Ask children to recall the animals the old woman swallowed and in what order they were eaten.

Have children practice the sample story. When they feel comfortable with the technique, have them work with a partner to create puppets for their favorite book and retell the story. (Templates for various characters are provided on pages 141–145.)

Have students write and create an original puppet story to share with the class.

Sample Story: "I Know an Old Lady Who Swallowed a Fly"

(an anonymous song)

I know an old lady who swallowed a fly.
I don't know why she swallowed a fly, I guess she'll die.

I know an old lady who swallowed a spider
That wiggled and jiggled and tickled inside her.
She swallowed a spider to catch the fly.
I don't know why she swallowed the fly, I guess she'll die.

I know an old lady who swallowed a bird.
How absurd to swallow a bird!
She swallowed the bird to catch the spider
That wiggled and jiggled and tickled inside her.
She swallowed the spider to catch the fly.
I don't know why she swallowed the fly, I guess she'll die.

I know an old lady who swallowed a cat.
Now fancy that, she swallowed a cat!
She swallowed the cat to catch the bird.
How absurd to swallow a bird!
She swallowed the bird to catch the spider
That wiggled and jiggled and tickled inside her.
She swallowed the spider to catch the fly.
I don't know why she swallowed the fly, I guess she'll die.

I know an old lady who swallowed a dog.
What a hog to swallow a dog!
She swallowed the dog to catch the cat.
Now fancy that, she swallowed a cat!
She swallowed the cat to catch the bird.
How absurd to swallow a bird!
She swallowed the bird to catch the spider
That wiggled and jiggled and tickled inside her.
She swallowed the spider to catch the fly.
I don't know why she swallowed the fly, I guess she'll die.

I know an old lady who swallowed a cow.
I don't know how she swallowed a cow.
She swallowed a cow to catch the dog.
What a hog to swallow a dog!
She swallowed the dog to catch the cat.
Now fancy that, she swallowed a cat!
She swallowed the cat to catch the bird.
How absurd to swallow a bird!

She swallowed the bird to catch the spider
That wiggled and jiggled and tickled inside her.
She swallowed the spider to catch the fly.
I don't know why she swallowed the fly, I guess she'll die.

I know an old lady who swallowed a horse.
She's dead, of course.

Books Appropriate for Puppet Stories for Grades K–2

Le Guin, Ursula K. *Fire and Stone*. New York: Atheneum, 1989. When the dragon comes swooping down breathing fire, only Min and Podo have the foresight to feed it what it wants. Sock puppet: dragon.

Martin, Bill. *Brown Bear, Brown Bear, What Do You See?* New York: Holt, 1967. Brown Bear sees a variety of animals, each one a different color. Face puppets: bear and other animals.

Scieszka, Jon. *The True Story of the Three Little Pigs*. New York: Viking, 1989. The wolf tells his own version of what really happened when he tangled with the three little pigs. Finger puppets: three pigs and wolf.

Books Appropriate for Puppet Stories for Grades 3–6

Grahame, Kenneth. *The Wind in the Willows*. New York: Viking, 1983. The adventures of four animal friends who live on a river bank in the English countryside. Face puppets: toad, mole, rat, badger.

Le Guin, Ursula K. *Catwings*. New York: Scholastic, 1988. Four young cats with wings leave the city slums in search of a better place to live. Stick puppets: four tabby cats with wings.

White, E. B. *Charlotte's Web*. New York: HarperCollins, 1980. Wilbur is a very lonely pig until a friendly spider teaches him about the meaning of friendship. Hand puppets: pig, spider, rat, and other barn animals.

Old Lady and the Figures She Swallows

Directions:

Figures are made on oaktag, colored and laminated or covered with clear vinyl plastic.

1. Enlarge the figure of the old lady or make a transparency and project it onto a piece of white oaktag. Adjust the projection to the size you want your old lady to be. Trace her outline.

2. Color in the old lady's hair and dress. Leave the rectangular area for her stomach white.

3. Tape a piece of heavy clear plastic over the front of the old lady and cut a slit in the oaktag near her shoulders to create a pocket with an opening in the back.

4. Make the other animal figures to fit inside the old lady's stomach and color them as you please.

5. When telling the story, place animal figures into the pocket using the slit in the back of the old lady.

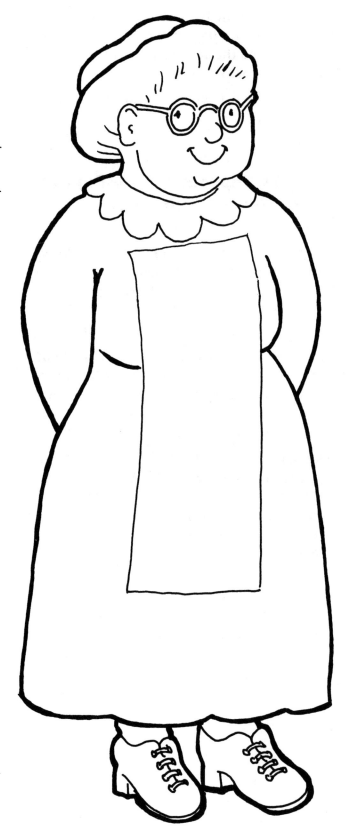

Figures for Old Lady

Figures for Old Lady

Face Puppets

Directions:
Make transparencies from figures. Tape oaktag on the wall. Project the transparencies on an overhead projector onto the oaktag the size you want. Draw the image and color it. Cover with clear contact paper or laminate and then cut out. Attach tongue depressors or popsicle sticks to the back of the face puppets to provide a handle.

Face Puppets

Finger Puppets

Directions:
Finger puppets can be made the same way as the face puppets on the previous pages, except that finger puppets need no handle.

Characters for Puppets

Directions:
These universal characters can be used to illustrate hundreds of stories. Make a transparency and project on an overhead projector onto oaktag on the wall. Color figures, adding special touches for specific stories. Cover with clear contact paper or laminate and then cut out. Attach sandpaper to the back to adhere to a felt board, or attach tongue depressors or popsicle sticks if you wish to use as stick puppets instead of felt figures.

Characters for Puppets

4

Chalk Talk Stories
"The North Wind and the Sun"
(grades 3–6),
"Tale of the Pink Pig" (grades K–2),
"The Surprise in the Playhouse"
(grades K–3),
My Side of the Mountain (grades 3–6)

Purpose

To have students:

- Work with a partner to retell the teacher's sample story.

- Draw conclusions from the story and discuss results.

- Create a chalk talk of a favorite story.

- Write and present an original chalk talk story.

Materials

Any of the following can be used:

chalkboard and chalk

whiteboard, mural paper, or chart paper with markers or crayons

overhead projector with transparencies

prop or character from book to wear on your hand as you draw

Activity

Explain that a chalk talk is a story that is drawn as it is told.

After you model the chalk talk, ask students to work with a partner to retell the story using paper and crayons. Each child should takes turns telling the story and drawing it.

Children then choose a favorite story and create their own chalk talk.

Then have children write an orginal story and present a chalk talk.

Sample Story:
"The North Wind and the Sun"

(adapted from an Aesop fable)

The North Wind and the Sun were fighting all day about who was the strongest. (*Draw Sun and North Wind.*)

To end their argument, they decided to see who could be the first to get a man out of his clothes. (*Draw man.*)

First the North Wind blew as hard as he could to blow the clothes off the man. However, this only made the man pull his clothes closer to him. So the North Wind gave up and told the Sun to give it a try. (*Draw North Wind blowing.*)

So the Sun beamed its warm rays and heated the air with bright sunshine. (*Erase Wind and draw Sun rays.*)

The man became very warm and took off his clothes. He decided to bathe in the sun. (*Erase man's scarf and top button. Draw shorts.*)

The moral of the story is: Persuasion is better than force.

Sample Story: "Tale of the Pink Pig"

(adapted from an anonymous tale)

(Use *pink* chalk or crayon for this chalk talk.)

One morning, Mary tumbled out of bed, very excited, just like this (*draw squiggle*). She was excited because her class was going to visit a farm that day.

She walked downstairs to have some breakfast, and she sat down at the table. She realized she had forgotten her juice, so she got up to get some apple juice and sat back down for a delicious breakfast of food that came from a farm. She ate eggs, wheat toast, and bacon. (*While telling story, draw as shown.*)

Mary looked at the clock and discovered that she was late, so she hurried back upstairs to her bedroom and ran down the hall to her bathroom just like this (*draw line from left to right*) to brush her teeth.

She went downstairs (*draw line downward*), but remembered that she had left her pencil upstairs. She went all the way back upstairs (*draw line up*), and had to come back down one more time (*draw another line down*).

On the way to school, Mary had to walk up a long, hilly, winding road like this one (*draw as shown*). She had to turn off the road to meet her friend, Bobby, who was going to the farm with her.

She went the wrong way at first, but then realized her mistake and quickly retraced her steps. She picked up Bobby, and the two of them headed back up the long, hilly, winding road towards school (*draw as shown*).

When they got to school, Mary and Bobby got on the bus and drove to the farm (*draw the ear*). On the way back, the bus got a flat tire, so they had to pull off to the side of the road like this and change it (*draw the eye*).

They continued on their way and made it back to school safely. Mary loved the class trip, so she ran all the way home to tell her mother about the farm. Guess what her favorite animal was!

Sample Story: "The Surprise in the Playhouse"

(adapted from an anonymous tale)

(In this story, the underlined words indicate when to draw.)

There was once a little girl named Lori, and there is an <u>L</u> for Lori. Lori found a great big empty refrigerator box one day outside a neighbor's house; it was left for the garbage man to pick up. Lori decided that the refrigerator box would make a terrific playhouse. She dragged the box home and set it in her backyard, and it looked <u>like this</u>.

The house needed a lot of work. The first thing Lori did was to <u>cut out two squares to make windows</u>, like this. Then she drew some <u>pretty shutters</u> that looked like these.

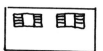

When she finished with the windows, <u>she cut out a door</u> just like this.

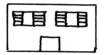

Lori wanted a way to get in and out of her house from the back. She thought about it a while and decided to make the back all open so it would feel bigger inside and a lot of light could shine in. To do this, <u>she cut the sides of the box, on both sides, down the middle and pulled the flaps open</u>. It made the house look like this.

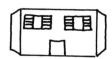

Lori found some tiny garden fencing in her garage. <u>She put the fence in front of her playhouse</u> and planted seeds behind the fence.

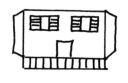

Now that her house was finished, she thought she'd go get her friend Linda. That's another <u>L</u> for Linda.

Linda lived across the street and down the block. So Lori skipped <u>across the street and went down the block</u> to Linda's house. <u>She went to the front door</u> and rang the bell.

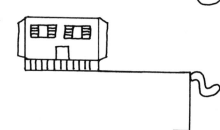

Linda's mother came to the door and said that Linda was upstairs in her room playing. <u>So Lori went upstairs</u> and asked Linda if she would like to see her new playhouse.

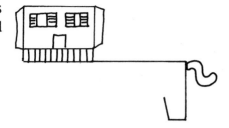

Linda said yes, so the <u>two girls hurried down the stairs</u>. Linda forgot her sweater so <u>she ran back up again</u> to get it. Now the girls were ready to go. <u>They went across the street</u> and were on their way back to Lori's house.

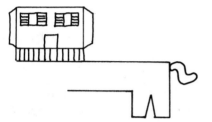

Lori stopped a minute and <u>bent down to look</u> at a caterpillar. Linda looked, too. <u>The girls got up and hurried along</u>. Then they pretended they were bunnies and <u>jumped up and down as they went. Lori fell down and Linda helped her up</u>.

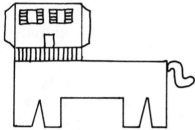

Soon they were at Lori's house. The girls were excited about playing in the playhouse. Just as Lori was about to say to Linda, "How do you like the house?" Linda stepped back and said, "Oh my, do you see the cute dog? Do you see it, Lori?

Sample Story: *My Side of the Mountain*

by Jean Craighead George (New York: Dutton, 1959)

For this chalk talk, you should use a boot hand prop (see page 154). Put the "boot" on your hand and use brown or gray chalk to draw the story. Follow the outline below for the introduction and quotes from the story and for a basic chalk talk to go with them. Ask the children why they think Sam Gribley is tired of living in the city, and ask them to make predictions about what happens to Sam on the mountain. Next, ask what they would bring with them if they were going to run away to a mountain. Discuss all of the responses and write or draw the children's responses on the board. When the chalk talk is over, encourage the children to create their own chalk talk from other parts of the book. Or they can create a chalk talk based on another survival or wilderness story they read, or maybe one that they wrote.

Sam Gribley lived in an apartment building with his dad, mother, four sisters, and four brothers. You can imagine how crowded their apartment must have been. (*Begin to draw city apartment buildings.*)

Sam was tired of New York City. He remembered how he always forgot his problems when he was in the woods. (*Finish drawing the city buildings.*)

Sometimes his dad would tell him of great-grandfather Gribley, who owned land in the Catskill Mountains. Sam knew that living in the wild was just the thing for a Gribley, so he left home and took the train north towards the Catskill Mountains. (*Draw a bumpy road and the front of a train.*)

Sam had brought with him his penknife, a ball of cord, an ax, and $40. He also had some flint and steel that he bought at a Chinese store in the city. (*Continue the bumpy road and draw these items along it.*)

Sam hitched rides up into the mountains, and he passed through a beautiful hemlock forest. "This is as far as I'm going," Sam said to the driver. Sam was on his side of the mountain, and it was only the beginning of his adventures. (*Draw the mountain.*)

Books Appropriate for Chalk Talks for Grades K–2

Carle, Eric. *The Very Busy Spider*. New York: Philomel, 1983.   An industrious spider continues to spin his web as the other farm animals try to distract him. Chalk talk: draw the spider's web as he spins it in the story.

Fleischman, Paul. *The Birthday Tree*. New York: HarperCollins, 1991.   A special tree reflects the events in a young man's life as his parents watch. Chalk talk: draw the tree and its branches, fruit, leaves, etc. as it goes through the changes in the story.

Johnson, Crockett. *Harold and the Purple Crayon*. New York: Harper and Row, 1955.   Chalk talk: use hand prop (see template on page 154) in telling story.

Krauss, Robert. *The Carrot Seed*. New York: Harper and Row, 1945.   Despite his family's lack of faith, a boy clings to his belief that the seed he had planted will grow. Chalk talk: draw a line for the ground, a watering can sprinkling water, and seedlings above the ground. Then gradually draw the shape of a carrot underground.

Books Appropriate for Chalk Talks for Grades 3–6

Choose the introduction or a favorite character, scene, or chapter from the book, or do a plot summary. Allow students to read a portion from the book or retell it in their own words. Some suggested characters for chalk talk drawings have been listed.

Alexander, Lloyd. *The Cat Who Wished to Be a Man*. New York: Dutton, 1973.   A wizard turns a cat into a man who begins to question humanity. Chalk talk: draw a cat.

Howe, James, and Deborah Howe. *Bunnicula*. New York: Atheneum, 1979.   A cat tries to warn his human family that their newfound baby bunny is a vampire. Chalk talk: draw a bunny.

Norton, Mary. *The Borrowers*. New York: Harcourt Brace, 1953.   An eccentric family keeps to itself until the daughter ventures out into the real world and makes a friend. Chalk talk: draw a girl and her friend.

Hand Props

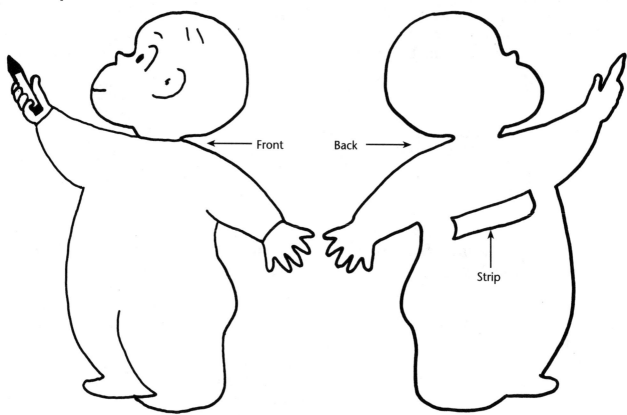

This figure of Harold, from *Harold and the Purple Crayon* by Crockett Johnson, can be slipped onto the chalk talk storyteller's hand to show Harold drawing his own story, or to be used as a symbol for chalk talks generally. The back of the figure has a strip of oaktag, fabric, or elastic to slip onto your hand.

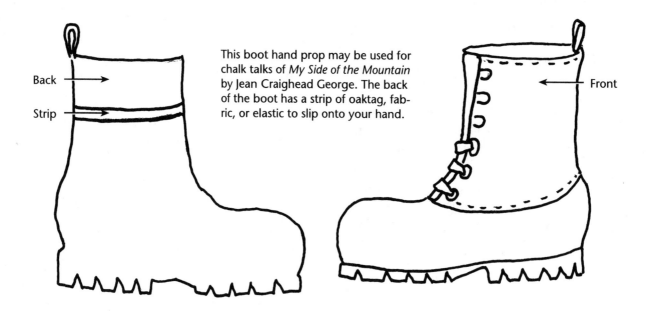

This boot hand prop may be used for chalk talks of *My Side of the Mountain* by Jean Craighead George. The back of the boot has a strip of oaktag, fabric, or elastic to slip onto your hand.

5

Photo Story

The Snowy Day (grades K–2)

Purpose

To have students:

- Retell the teacher's sample story to display an understanding of plot episodes using photographs.

- Retell a favorite story using photographs.

- Write, illustrate (with photos), and present an original story.

Materials

camera

film

props needed to act out story

Activity

Take photographs or slides of children acting out scenes from the story. If a video camera is available, you can videotape the students acting out the story. Then have the photographs or slides developed.

Explain that you are going to tell a story and use photos to illustrate it.

Tell the story and show the photos, slides, or video as you speak. You can show illustrations from the book side by side with the photos.

Have students retell the sample story using the photos, slides, or video.

Have students write, photograph, and present an original photo story.

Sample Story: *The Snowy Day*

by Ezra Jack Keats (New York: Viking, 1962)

Peter, the main character in the book, goes out into the snow and makes angels, builds a snowman, throws snowballs, and slides down a hill.

If you live where it snows, have a child dress in winter clothes and act out the previously described scenes (see photos). Props needed: jacket, boots, hat, scarf, mittens, stick.

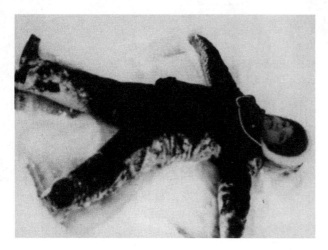 

A child reenacting scenes from *The Snowy Day* by Ezra Jack Keats; *left*, making angels in the snow, and *right*, making a snow man.

Books Appropriate for Photo Stories for Grades K–2

Borden, Louise. *Caps, Hats, Socks, and Mittens: A Book About the Four Seasons*. New York: Scholastic, 1988. Simple text and illustrations describe some of the pleasures of each season.

Zolotow, Charlotte. *Summer Is . . .* New York: Thomas Crowell, 1967. The beauty of summer, winter, fall, and spring.

———. *Hold My Hand*. New York: Harper and Row, 1972. Two little girls take a walk on a snowy day.

Books Appropriate for Photo Stories for Grades 3–6

Choose the introduction or a favorite scene or chapter from the book, or do a plot summary.

Byars, Betsy. *The Cybil War*. New York: Viking, 1981. Simon learns about friendship when his friend Tony's stories get him in trouble with Cybil, a girl he has a crush on.

Fitzhugh, Louise. *Harriet the Spy*. New York: Harper and Row, 1964. Harriet M. Welsh is an only child who doesn't get along with the other sixth graders. Forced to grow up with the loss of her nursemaid, she uses a notebook to record her thoughts.

Parish, Peggy. *Amelia Bedelia*. New York: Harper and Row, 1963. A clumsy yet lovable maid takes all of her job instructions literally.

6

Sound Stories

Charlie and the Chocolate Factory (grades 3–6),

"The Grouchy Queen and the Happy King" (grades K–2)

Purpose

To have students:

- Retell the teacher's sample story, with appropriate sounds.

- Retell a favorite story using sound effects for main characters.

- Write and present an original sound story.

Materials

Tape recorder

Activity

Tell students that they are to make certain sounds when you say certain names in the story.

Review the names and sounds and practice making the sounds. It will help to have both the names and the sounds written on a chart.

Tell the story and record it for use in the listening center.

Children retell the teacher's sample story and then create a sound story retelling of a favorite book.

Children write, illustrate, and present an original story.

Sample Story: *Charlie and the Chocolate Factory*

by Roald Dahl (New York: Knopf, 1973)

When the underlined words in the story are mentioned, the following sounds are made:

Mr. Wonka: Ha-ha-ha (he is always laughing and jolly).

Charlie Bucket: A sigh (he sighs a lot).

Augustus Gloop: Slirp-slirp (the sound of a dog lapping up water) (he gets in trouble drinking the chocolate river).

Veruca Salt: Cha-ching (the sound a cash register makes) (she is a spoiled little rich girl).

Violet Beauregarde: A chewing sound (she is always chewing gum).

Mike Teavee: Bang-bang (he always wears a holster with toy guns).

The following is a summary of Chapter 29.

"I wonder what happened to the others," said Mr. Wonka. The elevator neared the ground by the entrance of the chocolate factory. As Charlie looked out, he could see Augustus, Veruca, and Violet, and all of their parents. "But I only see three of them," said Charlie. "I expect Mike Teavee will be out very soon," replied Mr. Wonka. "Do you see the trucks, Charlie?"

Charlie answered yes and asked what they were for. Mr. Wonka replied, "The golden tickets said that each winner would get a lifetime supply of chocolate. The trucks will carry it home for them. Can you see Augustus Gloop?" continued Mr. Wonka. "There he is, getting into the truck with his parents."

"So he's really all right," asked Charlie, "even after going up the pipe?" "He's better than ever and skinnier than ever," replied Mr. Wonka.

"And there's Violet Beauregarde!" exclaimed Charlie. "I guess they were able to de-juice her. But what's wrong with Veruca Salt?" asked Charlie. "She's covered in garbage. Oh wait!" continued Charlie in amazement. "There's Mike Teavee. What did they do to him? He's so tall and thin."

"Oops!" replied Mr. Wonka. "They must have over-stretched him on the gum-stretching machine."

"That's terrible," said Charlie.

"Not true, Charlie," responded Mr. Wonka. "He's quite lucky. All of the professional basketball teams will want to recruit him."

"But now it's time we left these children," said Mr. Wonka. "I have something important to show you, Charlie." Mr. Wonka pressed another button and the elevator swooped up toward the sky.

Sample Story: "The Grouchy Queen and the Happy King"

(adapted from an anonymous tale)

When the underlined words in the story are mentioned, the following sounds are made:

Queen Grace the Grouch: Grrrrr.

King Happy Herman: Ha-ha-ha.

Whistling Wilbur: Whistling sound high to low.

Singing Sam: La-la-la (first few notes of "Mary Had a Little Lamb").

Tired Tim: Ahhhhh (yawning sound).

Lively Lorraine: Ah-ha.

Once upon a time there was a queen named Grace the Grouch. She had this name because she growled most of the time. Queen Grace the Grouch was married to King Happy Herman. He was called Happy Herman because he laughed most of the time. Together they made a perfect couple. Queen Grace the Grouch and King Happy Herman had three sons. The first son's name was Whistling Wilbur. He had this name because he whistled almost all the time. The second son's name was Singing Sam. He had this name because most of the time he sang. The third son's name was Tired Tim. He had this name because most of the time he was sleeping, and when he was awake he was doing almost nothing but yawning.

There was a princess from the next kingdom named Lively Lorraine. She couldn't sit still for a moment. She bounced around from dawn till dusk looking for things to do. Each time the princess would find a job to be done, she'd lift her hand in the air and say, "Ah-ha." When most people spoke of Lorraine, they could not help but say, "Ah-ha."

Lively Lorraine decided she'd like to marry. She knew of Queen Grace the Grouch and her husband, King Happy Herman. She also knew about their three sons, Whistling Wilbur, Singing Sam, and Tired Tim. Lively Lorraine decided to take a look at the three princes to see if one might be suitable for her as a future king. She saddled her horse one day and away she galloped to the kingdom over the hill.

When she arrived, she was greeted by Queen Grace the Grouch and her husband, King Happy Herman. Lively Lorraine decided to stay a while to get to know each prince and to see if there was one that best suited her.

First, Lively Lorraine played tennis with Whistling Wilbur. But he whistled so much throughout the game that Lively Lorraine could not concentrate and kept missing the ball.

The next day, Lorraine went sailing with Singing Sam. Sam was nice, but he never stopped singing. Instead of talking, he'd find an appropriate song and sing what he had to say. For a while it was fun, but Lorraine tired of it quickly.

Lively Lorraine felt sad. She decided that she would not meet the prince of her dreams here in this kingdom. But suddenly Tired Tim came yawning down the garden path. Lorraine took one look at him and said, "Ah-ha." Somehow Lively Lorraine and Tired Tim made the perfect couple—something like Queen Grace the Grouch and King Happy Herman.

So Lively Lorraine and Tired Tim trotted off to the kingdom over the hill to be married. Of course, they lived happily ever after.

Books Appropriate for Sound Stories for Grades K–2

Brown, Marcia. *The Noisy Book*. New York: HarperCollins, 1993. Muffin, the dog, is blindfolded for a day and tries to identify things by the sounds they make.

Seuss, Dr. (Theodore S. Geisel). *Mister Brown Can Moo! Can You?* New York: Random House, 1970. As Mr. Brown makes various sounds, children are encouraged to repeat them.

Books Appropriate for Sound Stories for Grades 3–6

Blume, Judy. *Superfudge*. New York: Dell, 1981. A young boy, Peter, describes the ups and downs of life with his younger brother, Fudge.

Herman, Charlotte. *Max Malone and the Great Cereal Rip-Off*. New York: Scholastic, 1990. Max is upset when the prize is missing from his cereal box, so he decides to investigate.

O'Brien, Robert C. *Mrs. Frisby and the Rats of N.I.M.H.* New York: Atheneum, 1971. Mrs. Frisby, a widowed mouse, turns to the wise rats for help in raising her children.

7

Music Story

The Three Little Pigs (grades K–2)

Purpose

To have students:

- Retell the teacher's sample story in order to discriminate between loud and soft sounds.

- Retell a favorite story using music to dramatize it.

- Write and present an original music story.

Materials

musical instruments

tape recorder

record player, etc.

Activity

Read the story and identify pieces of music that will represent each of the main characters.

Tell the story to the students and play the music (or play selections on the piano or other instrument) as you tell the story.

Tape the music so it is synchronized with the story.

Have children retell the sample story and then retell a favorite story using musical instruments of their choice.

Have them write and present an original music story.

Sample Story: *The Three Little Pigs*

by T. Izawa (New York: Grosset and Dunlap, 1970)

Retells the episode in the lives of two foolish pigs and how the third pig managed to avoid the same fate. A flute can be used for the sound of the pigs. Roll fingers across a keyboard or piano for the wolf.

Books Appropriate for Music Stories for Grades K–2

Brown, Marcia. *The Three Billy Goats Gruff*. New York: Harcourt Brace, 1957.   Tale of how three billy goats outwit a hungry troll.

160

Child, Lydia M. F. *Over the River and Through the Woods*. New York: Harper-Collins, 1993.   Illustrated version of a well-known song describing the joys of a visit to grandmother's house.

Duke, Kate. *Raffi Songs to Read: Tingalayo*. New York: Crown, 1989.   Illustrated version of a calypso song about a jovial donkey who befriends a girl at a Caribbean carnival.

Books Appropriate for Music Stories for Grades 3–6

Moss, Lloyd. *Zin! Zin! Zin! a Violin*. New York: Simon and Schuster, 1995.   Children meet the orchestra: trumpet, french horn, and other instruments.

Prokofiev, Sergei. *Peter and the Wolf*. New York: Viking, 1982.   Tale of a boy who, ignoring his grandfather's warnings, proceeds to capture a wolf. You can play the accompanying tape as you tell the story.

Rosenberg, Jane. *Play Me a Story*. New York: Knopf, 1994.   Children are introduced to classical music through various stories and poems.

8

Roll Movie Story

Little Red Riding Hood (grades K–2)

Purpose

To have students:

- Retell the teacher's sample story to identify details and plot episodes.

- Write and illustrate roll movie story of a favorite book.

- Write, illustrate, and present an original roll movie story.

Materials

white drawing or shelving paper

pencils, markers, crayons

tape

wooden dowels

self-adhesive vinyl

box

See directions for making roll movie box on page 164.

Activity

Tell the roll movie story, changing to a new scene when appropriate. The story should be written below each illustration or on the back.

Ask students to take note of the specific details and plot episodes chosen as pictures for the roll movie story.

At the completion of the roll movie story, read the actual book so that students can compare the two stories.

Explain that the roll movie is a shortened version of the original book. The story was retold in the teacher's own words, including the important details, plot episodes, and corresponding illustrations.

Have students work in small groups of three or four to create a roll movie story of a favorite book, followed by an original story to be shared with the class.

Sample Story: *Little Red Riding Hood*

by the Grimm Brothers (New York: Harcourt Brace, 1968)

A classic fairy tale of a little girl, her grandmother, and a wily wolf. Roll movie scenes:

1. Little Red Riding Hood in front of her cottage.

2. Red Riding Hood and her mother giving the girl a basket of food.

3. Red Riding Hood encountering wolf in forest.

4. Red Riding Hood picking flowers.

5. Red Riding Hood finding wolf in grandmother's bed.

6. Wolf in grandmother's clothes chasing Red Riding Hood.

7. Hunter chasing away the wolf.

8. Red Riding Hood, grandmother, and hunter drinking tea.

Books Appropriate for Roll Movie Stories for Grades K–2

Goble, Paul. *The Girl Who Loved Wild Horses*. Scarsdale, NY: Bradbury Press, 1978.   Though she is fond of her people, a girl prefers to live among the wild horses, where she is happy.

Keillor, Garrison. *Cat, You Better Come Home*. New York: Viking, 1995.   Puff, the cat, leaves home seeking a more extravagant lifestyle, but returns when she discovers life isn't greener on the other side.

Munsch, Robert N. *The Paper Bag Princess*. Toronto: Annick, 1980.   A princess outsmarts a dragon and gets rid of him for good. In the process she finds out it is better to be a smart princess than a well-dressed one.

Sendak, Maurice. *Where the Wild Things Are*. New York: Harper and Row, 1963. Max sails off in a private boat to where the wild things are and becomes their king.

Books Appropriate for Roll Movie Stories for Grades 3–6

Choose the introduction or a favorite scene or chapter from the book, or do a plot summary.

Juster, Norton. *The Phantom Tollbooth*. New York: Epstein and Carroll, 1961. Milo, a young boy, journeys through a land that cures his boredom with words and numbers.

O'Dell, Scott. *Island of the Blue Dolphins*. Boston: Houghton Mifflin, 1990.   A courageous Indian girl lives alone on an island for eighteen years, after her tribe emigrates and leaves her behind.

Paterson, Katherine. *Bridge to Terabithia*. Santa Barbara, CA: ABC-Clio, 1987.   A ten-year-old Virginia boy loses his new friend when she meets an untimely death trying to reach Terabithia, their hideaway, during a terrible storm.

Roll Movies

Making a roll movie is an excellent method for recording an original story. A roll movie box is an important piece of equipment for the classroom. With this device the child can write and illustrate his or her story and present the finished work to the class.

Directions:

1. Select a strong cardboard box about 18" high by 14" wide by 10" deep (45 cm x 35 cm x 25 cm).
2. Remove the cover or flaps of the box, leaving the sides and bottom.
3. Cut a rectangular shape out of the bottom of the box, leaving about 2" (5 cm) as a border on all sides.
4. Cut two holes on both sides of the box, close to the opening, yet far enough away to fit the roll of paper that will contain the illustrations (see diagram).
5. Obtain two wooden dowels about 20" (50 cm) long and place them through the holes in the box.
6. Cover the outside of the box with self-adhesive vinyl.
7. Draw each picture for the story on white shelving paper the right size to fit and show through the opening in the box. Write the text of the story under each illustration.
8. Turn the roll movie box to its back side, and attach the beginning of the roll to the top wooden dowel with masking tape. Roll up the pictures onto the top dowel and then attach the other end of the paper roll to the bottom dowel. Now roll the strip to its beginning position, and it is ready to be rolled and told.

Note: The movie box may be used horizontally, with the strip rolling onto the right-hand dowel. However, this may be more difficult, since the box cannot sit flat but must be held by someone or be placed on the edge of the table or desk.

Another idea: If you are lucky enough to have an old wooden TV frame, bore some holes and use it to show movie strips.

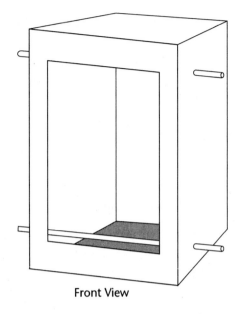

Front View

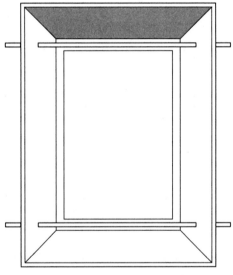

Back View

9
Movie Story

The Indian in the Cupboard
(grades 3–6)

Purpose

To have students:

- Retell stories that are movies made from books.
- Write original stories and retell them using a video camera.
- Discuss how books leave more to the imagination.

Materials

television

VCR

video of movie

copy of book

Activity

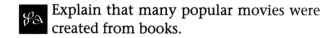 Explain that many popular movies were created from books.

After students have finished reading the book *The Indian in the Cupboard*, tell them that they will watch the movie.

Ask them to discuss the similarities and differences between the book and movie, which they liked better, and how books leave more to the imagination than movies.

Sample Story: *The Indian in the Cupboard*

by Lynne Reid Banks (New York: Doubleday, 1980)

In this story, a nine-year-old English boy accidentally brings his three-inch-tall Indian toy to life.

Appropriate Books That Are Also Movies for Grades K–6

Baum, L. Frank. *The Wizard of Oz.* New York: Holt, 1982. After a cyclone lands Dorothy in Oz, she must avoid the wicked witch and find her way back to Kansas.

Burnett, Frances Hodgson. *The Secret Garden.* New York: Holt, 1987. An orphan goes to live with her cold, unfeeling uncle. Behind his house she finds an abandoned garden.

Farley, Walter. *Black Stallion*. New York: Random House, 1961.   A young orphan boy is shipwrecked on a deserted island with a horse.

Lewis, C. S. *The Lion, the Witch, and the Wardrobe*. New York: Macmillan, 1970. Four children discover an empty wardrobe closet that leads to a magical kingdom filled with heroes and villains.

10

Television Story

Madeline (grades K–2)

Purpose

To have students:

- Increase motivation to read books after seeing television show.
- Identify similarities and differences between a book and the corresponding television program.

Materials

television

VCR

video of *Madeline*

copy of book

Activity

Show the video or find out when it will be shown on television and encourage children to watch.

Read the storybook to the class and ask students to identify the similarities and differences between the television show and the book.

Ask why things may have been left out or added to the television show compared to the book.

Discuss how books leave more to the imagination.

Sample Story: *Madeline*

by Ludwig Bemelmans (New York: Puffin, 1977)

Madeline charms her classmates with funny pranks. But when Madeline needs her appendix out, she's the one who needs charm and humor for a speedy recovery.

Appropriate Books That Are Also Television Programs for Grades K–6

Aardema, Verna. *Bringing the Rains to Kapiti Plain: A Nandi Tale*. New York: Dial, 1981.   A cumulative rhyme of how Ki-pat brought rain to the drought-stricken Kapiti Plain. (Reading Rainbow series)

Cole, Joanna. *The Magic School Bus Inside the Earth*. New York: Scholastic, 1987. Mrs. Frizzle and her magic school bus take her students into the earth for some real hands-on science explorations. (Reading Rainbow series)

————. *The Magic School Bus Inside Ralphie*. New York: Scholastic, 1995. Mrs. Frizzle and her magic school bus take her students into Ralphie's body to explore where his fever and sore throat are coming from. (Reading Rainbow series)

Food Story

"The Little Round Red House"
(grades K–2)

Purpose

To have students:

- Retell the teacher's sample story.

- Retell a favorite story using food as prop or to follow directions to make a recipe.

- Write and present an original food story.

Materials

apples

knife

Activity

 Tell the story "The Little Round Red House."

Cut the apple in half crosswise at the end to reveal the surprise.

Have students retell the sample story; have apples for snack.

Ask children to retell a story they know using a food prop, or make a recipe.

Have children write and present an original food story.

Sample Story: "The Little Round Red House"

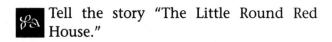

(adapted from an anonymous tale)

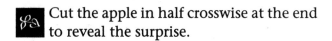

School had ended for the summer. Stephanie was wandering around the house trying to find something to do. She colored for a while, cut and pasted, and looked at some books; but nothing seemed like much fun today. She looked for her mother. Her mother was at her desk, busy with some important work.

Stephanie said to her mother, "What can I do today? I just can't seem to find anything."

Her mother thought for a while and said, "Stephanie, I know what you can do. Go outside for a walk and see if you can find a little round red house that has no windows and no doors, a chimney on top, and a star inside."

Stephanie wasn't really sure what her mother was talking about, but since it sounded interesting she decided to give it a try. First, Stephanie walked down Elm Street. Then she tried Heritage Lane. But not one house fit the description her mother had given. She could not find a little round red house that had no windows and no doors, a chimney on top, and a star inside. All the houses had windows and doors. None of the houses was even red.

When she was about to give up and go home, she met her friend Darren. He was looking for something to do. Stephanie asked him to help her with her search. The two children decided to ask Mr. and Mrs. Mandel if they knew of this little round red house. Mr. and Mrs. Mandel owned the candy shop in town, and they knew everything about the town in which Stephanie and Darren lived. If there was anyone who would know about such a strange house, it would be the Mandels.

Stephanie ran into the candy shop. She immediately asked Mrs. Mandel if she knew of a little round red house that had no windows and no doors, a chimney on top, and a star inside. Mrs. Mandel thought for a while and then said, "Stephanie, go down to the shady pond where the wind blows through the trees. Sit down a while to enjoy the summer day and the breeze rippling through the trees, and maybe you will find what you are looking for."

Darren and Stephanie hurried down to the shady pond. It was a long walk and the day was hot, so they were happy to sit down and rest by the pond in the shade of the trees. Before long, a lovely cool breeze blew through the branches of the trees. The leaves rustled, and something fell out of one of the trees.

Whatever fell bounced first on Stephanie's head and then fell to the ground. It had split into two pieces. Stephanie picked up the two pieces and put them back together again. Then she began to laugh. "My goodness," she said, "I've found it! This is the little round red house that has no windows and no doors, a chimney on top, and a star inside." Hungry from their experience, Darren and Stephanie each took a piece and enjoyed the *apple* (*show cut apple*) that had fallen from the tree.

Books Appropriate for Food Stories for Grades K–2

Bond, Felicia. *If You Give a Mouse a Cookie*. New York: HarperCollins, 1985.   A boy meets a mouse who will do anything for a cookie.

Flemming, Denise. *Lunch*. New York: Holt, 1992.   A very hungry mouse eats a large lunch comprised of colorful foods.

McCloskey, Robert. *Blueberries for Sal*. New York: Viking, 1948.   A bear cub and a little girl wander off from their mothers to pick blueberries and end up confusing each other's mothers for their own.

The Little Round Red House

Cut apple on the dotted line.

Books Appropriate for Food Stories for Grades 3–6

Bailey, Carolyn S., and Clara M. Lewis. *Favorite Stories for the Children's Hour.* New York: Platt and Munk, 1965. "How Maple Sugar Came," an Indian legend, and "The Wonderful Porridge Pot," from the Brothers Grimm.

Barrett, Judy. *Cloudy with a Chance of Meatballs.* New York: Atheneum, 1978. Life is delicious in the town of Chewandswallow, where it rains soup and juice, snows mashed potatoes, and blows storms of hamburgers, until the weather takes a turn for the worse.

Sendak, Maurice. *Chicken Soup with Rice.* New York: Harper and Row, 1962. A nonsensical rhyming book about the months of the year and chicken soup.

Books with Recipes to Cook

Blume, Judy. *Freckle Juice.* New York: Macmillan, 1971. Pupils in grades 2–5, especially those with freckles, will enjoy this book. Nicky has freckles all over. Andrew wishes he had freckles. Sharon offers Andrew her recipe for freckle juice. Andrew mixes the recipe and the unexpected happens.

Recipe: Freckle Fruit Punch

To make 35 servings you will need: 3 qts. unsweetened pineapple juice; juice of 8 oranges; juice of 4 lemons; 2 cups sugar; 4 qts. ginger ale; 2 qts. plain soda water; 1 pint fresh strawberries, quartered.

Combine juices and sugar and chill thoroughly. Just before serving add ginger ale, soda water, and strawberries.

Calhoun, Mary. *The Witch of Hissing Hill.* New York: William Morrow, 1967. Primary children will enjoy this story about Sizzle, a witch famous for her black cats. One of her cats gives birth to a good witch cat. Sizzle is horrified and tries to get rid of it. In the end, all of Sizzle's cats become good cats.

Recipe: Sizzle and Gold's Love Medicine

To make 24 servings, you will need two 2-liter bottles of root beer soda and 1/2 gallon vanilla ice cream.

Cover a large kettle with black paper to resemble a witch's cauldron. Pour the chilled soda into the kettle and drop in scoops of ice cream. Stir and serve.

Dahl, Roald. *Charlie and the Chocolate Factory.* New York: Knopf, 1973. Everyone, especially those who have seen the movie, will enjoy the adventures of Charlie Bucket, a poor boy who lives next to Willy Wonka's wonderful chocolate factory. Charlie wins a ticket for a tour of the factory; his adventures there are hilarious.

Recipe: Charlie's Chocolate Flake Candy

For six dozen pieces, you will need: 5 cups cornflakes; 1/4 tsp. salt; 1 lb. sweet milk chocolate; 2 1-oz. squares unsweetened chocolate.

Combine cornflakes and salt. Melt the chocolates together in a double boiler; pour over cornflake mixture; mix well, slightly crushing the cornflakes. Drop from teaspoon onto waxed paper. Chill several hours. Keep in cool place.

Devlin, Harry, and Wende Devlin. *Cranberry Thanksgiving.* New York: Parent's Magazine Press, 1971. Maggie and her grandmother live by a cranberry bog. Maggie's grandmother is famous for her cranberry bread, and is said to make the best for miles around. On Thanksgiving both Maggie and her grandmother invite a guest to dinner. When the meal is over, Maggie's grandmother learns a lesson about judging people by how they look.

Recipe: Grandma's Famous Cranberry Bread

To make one loaf of bread, you will need: 2 cups all-purpose flour; 1 cup sugar; 1 1/2 tsp. baking powder; 1 tsp. salt; 1/2 tsp. baking soda; 1/4 cup butter or margarine; 1 egg, beaten; 1 tsp. grated orange peel; 3/4 cup orange juice; 1 cup coarsely chopped walnuts; 1 1/2 cups fresh or frozen cranberries, chopped.

Combine flour, sugar, baking powder, salt, and baking soda in a large bowl. Cut in butter until mixture is crumbly. Add egg, orange peel, and orange juice all at once; stir just until mixture is evenly moist. Fold in cranberries and nuts. Spoon into a greased 9" x 5" x 3" loaf pan. Bake at 350°F for one hour and 10 minutes, or until a toothpick inserted in the center comes out clean. Remove from pan and cool on wire rack. Slice and serve.

Hader, Berta, and Elmer Hader. *The Big Snow.* **New York: Macmillan, 1948.** As the geese fly south, the animals recognize this as a sign that winter is coming. A big snow falls and covers the ground. The animals can no longer find food. Then a little old woman scatters seeds, nuts, and bread crumbs for them.

Recipe: Pinecone Bird Feeder

Each pupil will need one large pinecone. Also needed are a large jar of peanut butter, birdseed, and string.

Spread the peanut butter into the open spaces of a pinecone. Stick birdseed into the peanut butter. Tie a string to the pinecone and hang it on a tree at home or outside the classroom.

Ipcar, Dahlov. *Hard Scrabble Harvest.* **New York: Doubleday, 1976.** This story for young readers relates in rhyme the farmers' struggle against the possibility of bad weather and pesky insects, from spring planting to fall harvest. Happily, the book ends with a harvest of tomatoes, apples, pumpkins, and corn.

Recipe: Pumpkin Pie

To make one 9" pie, you need: 1 1/2 cups cooked or canned pumpkin; 3/4 cup sugar; 1/2 tsp. salt; 1/4 tsp. nutmeg; 3 eggs, slightly beaten; 1 1/4 cup milk; 3/4 cup evaporated milk; one uncooked 9" pie shell.

Combine pumpkin, sugar, salt, and spices. Add eggs and milk, and cream together. Pour into the unbaked pie shell. Bake in a hot oven (425°F) for 10 minutes, then in a moderate oven (325°F) for another 45 minutes or until the mixture does not adhere to a knife inserted in the middle.

Keats, Ezra Jack. *The Snowy Day.* **New York: Viking, 1962.** On the first snowy day of winter, everyone will enjoy the adventures of a boy who goes out to play in the newly fallen snow. He builds a snowman, makes angels, throws snowballs, and takes a snowball into his house to save for the next day.

Recipe: Ice Cream Snowballs

To make 25 snowballs you will need: 1/2 gallon vanilla ice cream; 2 cups shredded coconut.

Scoop 25 round ice cream balls. Roll in shredded coconut. Put into freezer.

Lawson, Robert. *Rabbit Hill.* **New York: Viking, 1944.** A good story for middle elementary grades. The rabbit family and its friends worry if the people moving into the big house near their rabbit hill will be mean and pinching, or folks with a thought for the small creatures who have always lived there. The new folk prove their beneficence to animals by planting their vegetable garden without fences.

Recipe: Rabbit Hill Spring Salad

If possible, use ingredients from a vegetable garden planted by the class. To make 25 servings you will need: 2 heads lettuce; 2 cucumbers; 2 stalks celery; 1 bunch carrots; 1 dozen tomatoes.

Wash all vegetables. Tear lettuce into small pieces; slice cucumbers, celery, carrots, and tomatoes. Place each ingredient in its own separate bowl. Children take a dish and serve themselves salad bar style.

Lenski, Lois. *Strawberry Girl*. **New York: Lippincott, 1945.** Use this story with middle elementary graders. Birdie Boyer's family has moved to Florida's backwoods to raise small crops of sweet 'taters, strawberries, oranges, and the like.

Recipe: Strawberry Layer Dessert

To make 12 servings, you will need: 1 10-oz. pkg. frozen sliced strawberries (thawed); 1 3-oz. pkg. strawberry gelatin; 1 cup hot water; 1 cup whipping cream (whipped); 1 10-inch tube angel cake.

Drain strawberries, reserving 1/2 cup syrup. Dissolve gelatin in hot water. Add reserved syrup. Chill until partially set. Beat mixture till light and fluffy. Fold in whipped cream. Chill until of spreading consistency. Transfer 1 1/2 cups mixture to small bowl; fold in drained strawberries. Split cake crosswise into three equal layers. Fill between layers with strawberry mixture. Frost top and sides with remaining whipped-cream mixture. Chill and serve.

Lobel, Anita. *The Pancake*. **New York: William Morrow, 1978.** This story of the adventures of a pancake who rolls away when overhearing that he is about to be eaten will appeal to primary children. The pancake escapes the woman, her seven children, a farmer, a goose, a cat, a goat . . . but not the pig.

Recipe: M&M Pancakes

For 12 pancakes you will need: 2 cups pancake mix; 1 cup milk; 2 eggs; 1 tbs. oil or melted shortening; 1 large pkg. M&M's.

Preheat and lightly grease a griddle. Put pancake mix, milk, eggs, and shortening in a bowl. Stir until smooth. Pour batter onto hot griddle in small circles. Turn pancakes when tops cover with bubbles. Let children decorate with M&M's.

Mariana. *Miss Flora McFlimsey's Valentine*. **New York: Lothrop, Lee and Shepard, 1967.** Primary children will like this book. Miss Flora's wish to make surprise valentines for her friends in the forest is almost spoiled by one of the animals. All ends well with valentine treats.

Recipe: Valentine Surprise

For 8 to 10 servings, you will need: 1 large pkg. of cherry gelatin; 1 jar cherry pie filling; 1/2 cup sour cream; 1 8-oz. pkg. cream cheese; 1/2 cup sugar; 1 tsp. vanilla.

Make gelatin according to directions on package. Mix in cherry pie filling. Put in an 8 1/2" x 11" flat dish. Cream together sour cream, cream cheese, sugar, and vanilla. Spread on top of gelatin. Chill and serve.

McCloskey, Robert. *Blueberries for Sal*. **New York: Viking, 1948.** Primary children will have fun with this story. One summer day a little girl and her mother, as well as a bear cub and his mother, set out for a blueberry search in Maine. While hiking up opposite sides of a hill, the two children stray from their blueberry-picking mothers. The children are concerned only with filling themselves full of fruit.

Recipe: Blueberry Muffins

For 15 large muffins you will need: 1 stick butter; 1 cup sugar; 2 eggs; 1 cup flour; 1 tsp. baking powder; 1 tsp. vanilla; 1 cup blueberries.

Cream the butter and sugar. Add eggs and beat. Add flour, baking powder, and vanilla. Mix well. Fold in blueberries gently. Drop mixture into foil baking cups. Bake 25 minutes, or until muffins are golden brown, at 350°.

York, Carol. *Johnny Appleseed*. **New York: Troll, 1980.** Middle graders will appreciate this story about Johnny Appleseed's adventures as a pioneer, and how he wandered through the West planting his apple seeds.

Recipe: Applesauce

To make 12 servings, you will need: 12 apples (1 medium apple per serving); water; 6 tbs. sugar.

Cut apples into quarters; remove cores and stems, and pare. Place in deep saucepan. Add water until it can be seen in the spaces between the apples. Cover and cook until tender (about 20 to 30 minutes). Add sugar and continue cooking until it dissolves. Mash and stir apples until they are the desired consistency.

Zolotow, Charlotte. *Mister Rabbit and the Lovely Present*. New York: Harper and Row, 1962.   Primary children will find a kinship with this little girl who tries to decide upon a birthday present for her mother and asks the help of a rabbit. Together they choose an apple, a banana, a pear, and grapes for the birthday present.

Recipe: Mr. Rabbit's Fruit Ambrosia

For 6 servings you will need: 2 bananas; bunch of blue grapes; 2 apples; 2 green pears; 1/2 cup confectioner's sugar; 2 cups shredded coconut.

Peel and cut bananas, apples, and pears into small slices. Cut grapes in half and remove pits if necessary. Combine sugar and coconut. Arrange alternate layers of bananas, apples, pears, and grapes in a glass serving dish. Sprinkle each layer with the sugar-coconut mixture, including the top. Chill and serve.

12

Cut Story

"The Unusual House" (grades 3–6)

Purpose

To have students:

- Retell the teacher's sample story.
- Retell a favorite story using the cut technique.
- Write and present an original cut story.

Materials

scissors

colored construction paper

pencils

Activity

Explain that while you tell a story, you will cut out pictures of characters or figures that go along with the story.

Students practice until they can retell the sample story while cutting out the figures.

Children work with a partner to retell a favorite story while using the cut story technique.

Children write and present an original cut story.

Sample Story: "The Unusual House"

(adapted from an anonymous tale)

(Take a piece of construction paper and fold it in half lengthwise; draw the outline of half a flower, as shown in the illustration. As you tell the story, cut out the flower.)

Near Susan's house was a wooded area. Once in a while Susan and her mother would walk through the woods together, exploring. Susan's mother told her never to go into the woods alone because she might get lost. Susan was allowed, however, to play in the grassy field at the edge of the woods.

While Susan was playing in the field one day, a butterfly with many colors attracted her attention. She chased it through the field, and before she realized it she was in the woods, running after the fast butterfly. Finally the butterfly landed, and Susan got a good look at it. It was pink, white, and blue. It was very beautiful. It flew off again, but this time Susan didn't chase it. She was tired from all the running she had just done. She sat down on a rock and watched the butterfly circle overhead. It finally flew farther and farther overhead, until Susan could see it no longer. (*Begin cutting, but do not unfold.*)

When she caught her breath, Susan looked around and, to her surprise, she saw that she was deep in the woods. She could not see the clearing anywhere. She got up and started for the grassy field but really wasn't sure which way to go. She began walking in the direction she thought was right. She walked straight ahead for a while, around some bushes, up a short hill, and down a path. She went around this way and that, up and down and around, but still could not find her way out. She thought she might be lost forever. She sat down on a rock and was about to cry when in the distance she noticed a house with a very strange shape. The house was most unusual; it looked something like this. (*Display the folded cutout half flower.*)

Susan was frightened but didn't know where else to go. She walked slowly toward the house and noticed that it had a most unusual chimney that was shaped something like this. (*Hold up and show cutout chimney piece.*)

Susan's curiosity got the best of her, and she continued straight for the house. She noticed that the door of the house was as unusual as the chimney and had a shape that looked something like this. (*Hold up and show cutout door piece.*)

As she got even closer to the strange-shaped house, she could see its windows. There were only two, and they were both shaped something like this. (*Hold up and show cutout window piece.*)

Susan's curiosity again got the best of her. She moved toward the house carefully and quietly. When she was about to get to the front door, she suddenly became frightened again. At that very moment something touched her on the shoulder. She turned quickly to see what it was. It was a beautiful flower! (*Unfold the cutout.*) It smiled and said:

Happy spring day!

Don't run away.

The nice people in the house

Would like you to stay.

Susan knocked on the door of the house. The people inside the house were nice, so Susan stayed a while and played. After giving her some cookies and milk, the people told Susan how to get home. She arrived at her own house safe and sound, with a beautiful flower to give to her mother.

This same story can be told at other times of the year. Instead of cutting out a flower shape, cut an autumn leaf in the fall, a pumpkin for Halloween, a Christmas tree at Christmas time, a valentine for Valentine's Day, and a shamrock for St. Patrick's Day (see figures). As you change the item being cut in the story, change the first line of the rhyme "Happy spring day!" to "Happy Valentine's Day!" "Happy Halloween Day!" and so on.

If you develop simple fold drawings of a boy, a girl, a rabbit, a house, a tree, and so on, you will be able to tell many stories with the cut technique.

Sample Cut Story Art

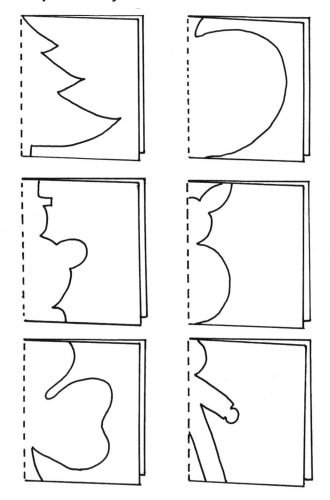

Books Appropriate for Cut Stories for Grades K–2

Charles, Françoise. *Jean Marie Counts Her Sheep*. New York: Scribner's, 1951. Fold eleven pieces of construction paper. On each, draw sheep with their backs on the fold. As Jean Marie dreams of getting each new sheep, cut out another and open it up so that it stands.

Holdsworth, William. *Gingerbread Boy*. New York: Farrar, Straus and Giroux, 1968.   Fold, draw, and cut out half a gingerbread boy and the characters he meets along his way.

Books Appropriate for Cut Stories for Grades 3–6

King-Smith, Dick. *Babe the Gallant Pig*. New York: Random House, 1983.   Draw a pig with its back on the fold. Cut it out as you tell the story so that the pig stands up. Cut out the other farm animals named in the story.

Silverstein, Shel. *The Giving Tree*. New York: Harper and Row, 1964.   From a folded piece of paper, cut out a tree with branches and open up the paper. Put several pieces of red paper together and cut out apples as you tell about the boy eating the tree's apples. When the tree gives the boy its branches, cut the branches off your tree. When the tree gives the boy its trunk, cut the trunk off the tree, leaving a small stump.

13

Origami Story

Swimmy (grades K–2)

Purpose

To have students:

- Retell the teacher's sample story in order to understand and identify the story characters.

- Retell a favorite story using the origami technique.

- Write an original story and make an origami character.

Materials

paper (newspaper, construction paper, or tissue paper)

Activity

Practice folding origami figures until you feel confident with the technique and can fold and tell the story smoothly. (See list of books on origami and paper-folding techniques below.)

While telling the story, fold the paper into the main character or object and display it until the story is ended.

Sample Story: *Swimmy*

by Leo Lionni (New York: Knopf, 1963)

A little black fish escapes being eaten by a giant tuna and finds comfort and safety in numbers with his new friends. Origami technique: Fold paper into the shape of a fish (see sample fish on page 181).

Books Appropriate for Origami Stories for Grades K–2

G'ag, Wanda. *Millions of Cats*. New York: Coward-McCann, 1956. An enchanting tale of a gentle peasant who goes off in search of one kitten and returns with "hundreds of cats, thousands of cats, millions and billions and trillions of cats." Origami figure: cat.

Lear, Edward. *The Owl and the Pussycat*. New York: Holiday House, 1983. After a courtship voyage of a year and a day, Owl and Pussycat finally buy a ring from Piggy and are blissfully married. Origami figure: boat.

Oppenheim, Joanne. *Have You Seen Birds?* New York: Scholastic, 1968. Inventively illustrated, a tale about birds of all kinds. Origami figure: bird (see instructions on page 182).

Books Appropriate for Origami Stories for Grades 3–6

Cleary, Beverly. *The Mouse and the Motorcycle*. New York: William Morrow, 1965. A reckless young mouse makes friends with a boy in a motel and discovers the joy of motorcycling. Origami figure: mouse.

Coerr, Eleanor. *Sadako and the Thousand Paper Cranes*. New York: Dell, 1977. Based on a true story of a Japanese girl who died of leukemia at the age of 12—the result of the radiation from the bomb dropped on Hiroshima where she lived during World War II. Legend says if sick people fold 1,000 paper cranes, the gods will make them well. Sadako folded 644 cranes before she died; her classmates folded the rest (see sample origami paper crane).

Naylor, Phyllis Reynolds. *Shiloh*. New York: Atheneum, 1991. A boy finds a lost beagle and tries to hide it from his family and the real owner. Origami figure: dog (see instructions on page 183).

Steig, William. *Sylvester and the Magic Pebble*. New York: Simon and Schuster, 1969. Sylvester Duncan, the donkey, finds a magic pebble that grants wishes. Origami figure: donkey.

Teacher Resources on Origami

Arika, Chiyo. *Origami in the Classroom*, vols. 1 and 2. Rutland, VT: Charles E. Tuttle, 1965–68.

Harbin, Robert. *New Adventures in Origami*. New York: Harper and Row, 1971.

Honda, Isao. *The World of Origami*. Tokyo and San Francisco: Japan Publications Trading Co., 1965.

Lang, Robert J. *Origami Animals: Paper Animals from Around the World*. New York: Crescent, 1992.

Murray, William, and Francis Rigney. *Paper Folding for Beginners*. New York: Dover, 1960.

Randlett, Samuel. *The Best of Origami*. New York: Dutton, 1968.

Rojas, Hector. *Origami Animals*. New York: Sterling, 1993.

Origami Fish

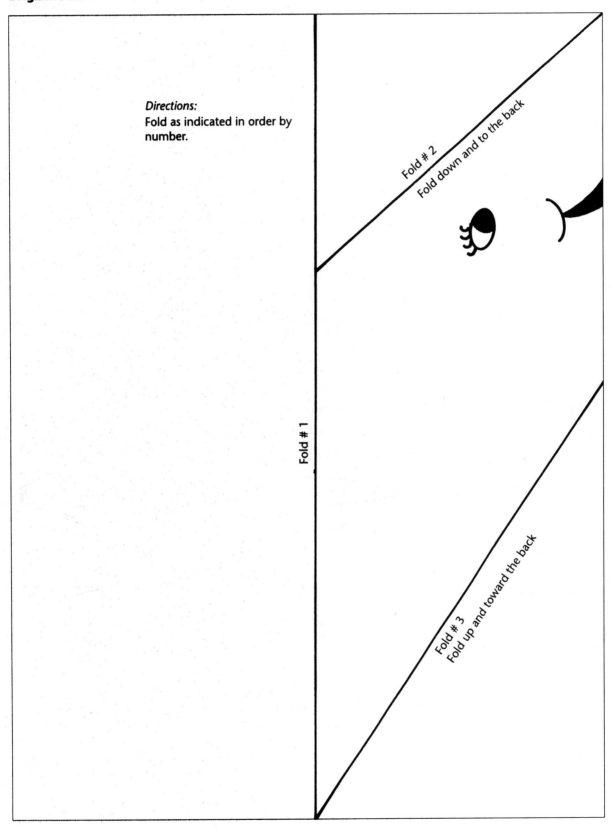

Directions:
Fold as indicated in order by number.

Fold # 2
Fold down and to the back

Fold # 1

Fold # 3
Fold up and toward the back

Origami Crane

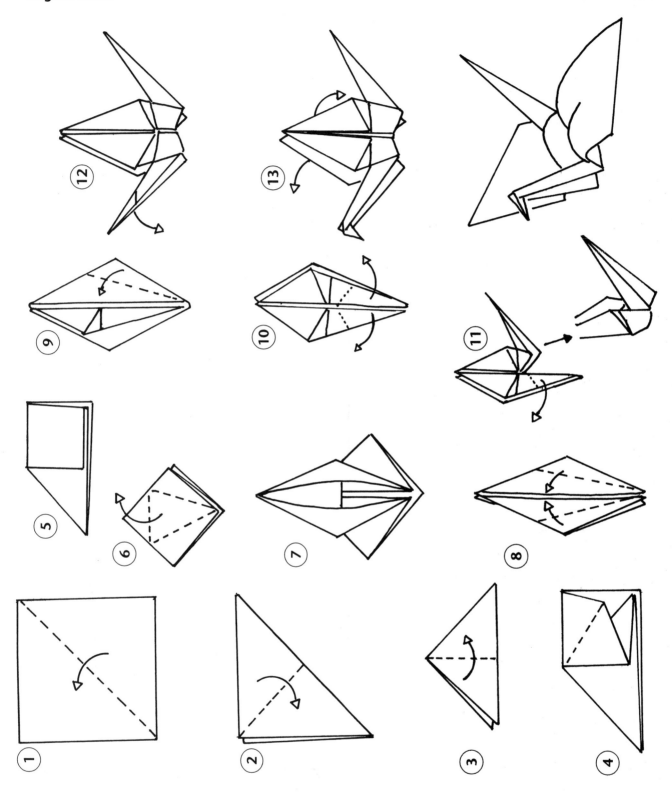

Origami Puppy from *Origami Magic* by Florence Temko (New York: Scholastic, 1993)

Directions
You will need two squares of construction paper, about 6" (15 cm) each—one for the head, and one for the body.

Head (use one square)
1. Fold corner to corner. Unfold paper flat.
2. Fold top corner to bottom corner.
3. Fold both outside corners to the crease.
4. Push your finger inside one triangle and spread it apart. Press it flat into a square. Repeat on the other side.
5. Fold up the bottom corner, one layer of paper only.

Body (use the other square)
1. Fold up tip of one corner. Turn paper over to the other side.
2. Fold corner to corner.
3. Pull the corner away and crease the tail to stay in place.

Assembly
Place the head on top of the body.

Head

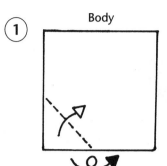

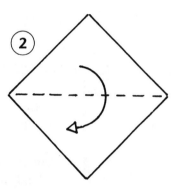

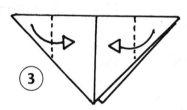

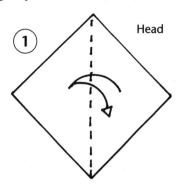

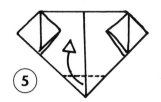

Body

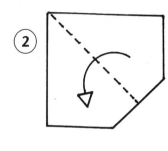

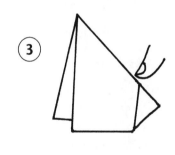

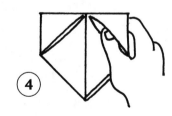

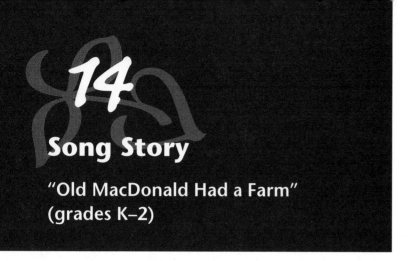

14
Song Story

"Old MacDonald Had a Farm"
(grades K–2)

Purpose

To have students:

- Retell the teacher's sample story.
- Notice syllables in the musical beat.
- Create story songbooks.

Materials

copies of "Old MacDonald Had a Farm" by Robert Quackenbush (New York: Lippincott, 1972), "Go Tell Aunt Rhody" by Robert Quackenbush (New York: Lippincott, 1973), and *Chicken Soup with Rice* by Maurice Sendak (New York: Harper and Row, 1962.)

white paper

colored construction paper

stapler

felt tip pens and crayons

Activity

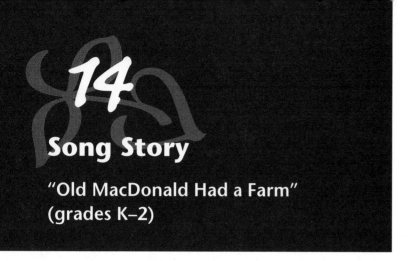 Read "Old MacDonald Had a Farm."

Sing the song and show the pictures in the book.

Do the same with "Go Tell Aunt Rhody" and *Chicken Soup with Rice*.

Discuss other songs that children could make into books.

Have children work in pairs to create their own songbooks.

Books Appropriate for Song Stories for Grades K–6

Keats, Ezra Jack. *Over in the Meadow*. New York: Four Winds Press, 1972.

Quackenbush, Robert. *She'll Be Coming 'Round the Mountain*. New York: Lippincott, 1973)

Spier, Peter. *The Erie Canal*. New York: Doubleday, 1970.

Part 3

All About Books

This section is meant to provide teachers of grades K–6 with activities that will enable students to develop literacy concepts and that will encourage them to apply this knowledge to reading and writing. All of the storytelling techniques provided in the previous section can be used in conjunction with the activities presented in this section and serve as a vehicle for students to share their literacy learning. The following activities promote independent and voluntary reading, introduce an author and illustrator study, and develop students' understanding of various genres.

Introduction to Quiet Book Time

Purpose

To demonstrate Quiet Book Time for independent reading.

Materials

classroom library's collection of books

Activity

Explain what Quiet Book Time is. Tell children that when it is Quiet Book Time, they are to select one or two books from the literacy center and find a quiet place in the classroom where they feel comfortable reading or looking at their books independently.

2
Writing to Authors

Purpose

To have students:

- Realize authors are real people.

- Extend understanding of letter writing as a means of communication.

Materials

writing paper

pens, pencils, crayons

several copies of familiar literature books

sample letter

Activity

Show children the books and read their titles.

Ask if anyone is familiar with the author and if anyone knows the titles of any other books by that author.

Explain that the authors who write the stories in books are real people.

Have children select one of their favorite authors and write a letter to the author telling him or her what they liked about one or more of the author's books. Remind students to include questions they would like answered about the book or the author.

Have children illustrate in the letter their favorite or the funniest part of the book(s) they are writing about.

Give a copy of the following letter to any child who cannot write independently and allow him or her to use it.

Dear_____,

I have been reading many books. I like one of yours very much. The title of the book is _____.

How do you get ideas for books?

I am sending you a picture of my favorite part of the book.

Please answer this letter. I have never met an author.

Sincerely,

Address envelopes to the publishers, and mail the letters. Share any responses with the children as they come in.

188

3
Series Book Author Study

Purpose

- To have students understand who authors are and what they do.

- To introduce series books and examine authors' writing styles.

Materials

copies of Ludwig Bemelmans' *Madeline* (New York: Puffin, 1977), about a young girl named Madeline as she experiences life in a boarding school; and *Madeline's Rescue* (New York: Penguin, 1981), about how Madeline's life is saved by a dog who later stirs up a great deal of trouble in her school

copies of Katherine Holabird's *Angelina Ballerina* (New York: Random House, 1992), about a forgetful young mouse named Angelina, who dreams of becoming a ballerina; and *Angelina's Birthday Surprise* (Santa Barbara, CA: ABC-Clio, 1990), in which Angelina discovers what a special day a birthday can be.

copies of Bill Martin's *Brown Bear, Brown Bear, What Do You See?* (New York: Holt, 1967), in which children see a variety of

different animals that are different colors; and *Polar Bear, Polar Bear, What Do You See?* (New York: Holt, 1991), in which children are encouraged to listen and imitate zoo animals' distinctive sounds

Activity

Hold a brief class discussion about what students think an author does.

Explain that all authors have their own writing style and some authors have particular topics they write about in what is known as a series style.

Read a page from four books by two different authors and ask children to guess which two books are written by the same author. Students should listen for similar character names and the general writing style of the author.

Allow children to look through their classroom library to find series books and share their findings with the class.

Series Books for Grades K–2

Alexander, Sue. *World Famous Muriel*. New York: Little, Brown, 1984. Muriel, a tight-rope walker, solves the mystery of the queen's missing lanterns.

——. *World Famous Muriel and the Scary Dragon*. New York: Little, Brown, 1985. When a dragon becomes a threat to the kingdom, Muriel thinks up a plan to keep everyone happy.

Bridwell, Norman. *Clifford, the Big Red Dog*. New York: Scholastic, 1963. Emily Elizabeth tells about her adventures with her big red dog.

——. *Clifford's Puppy Days*. New York: Scholastic, 1989. Fun memories of Clifford's days as a puppy.

Brown, Marcia. *Arthur's Baby*. New York: Joy Street, 1987. To Arthur's dismay, his parents' big surprise is not a new bicycle, but a new baby.

——. *Arthur's Birthday*. New York: Joy Street, 1989. Arthur's birthday party plans must undergo some changes when he hears that his friend Muffy's party is the same day.

Series Books for Grades 3–6

Cleary, Beverly. *Henry and Beezus*. New York: Avon Camelot Books, 1990. Henry Higgins thinks his friend Beezus's sister Ramona is a pest until she helps Beezus save money for a bicycle.

——. *Ramona the Pest*. New York: Avon Camelot Books, 1992. Ramona Quimby's adventures in kindergarten lead to her dropping out.

Hurwitz, Johanna. *The Up and Down Spring*. New York: Scholastic, 1994. Rory and Derek's friend Bolivia plans many activities for spring break, but they end up backfiring.

——. *The Hot and Cold Summer*. New York: Scholastic, 1995. Derek befriends a girl named Bolivia.

MacLachlen, Patricia. *All the Places to Love*. New York: HarperCollins, 1994. A young boy describes the favorite places that he shares with his family on his grandparents' farm and in the nearby countryside.

——. *Baby*. New York: Delacorte, 1993. While taking care of a baby that was left with them at the end of the tourist season, a family is able to come to terms with the death of their own infant.

4

Illustrator Study

Purpose

To have students:

- Understand what an illustrator does.

- Increase their visual discriminatory skills by noticing the differences and similarities among different illustrators.

- Appreciate and explore different artistic media.

Materials

watercolors, pastels, colored pencils

collage materials

pencils

paper

transparencies from selected books

copies of Eric Carle's *A House for a Hermit Crab* (New York: Scholastic, 1991), in which a hermit crab is helped and helps others through the changes he goes through; and *The Very Quiet Cricket* (New York: Philomel, 1990), in which a small cricket tries to greet his fellow insect friends but has a difficult time chirping (artistic style: watercolor/collage)

copies of Anthony Brown's *The Tunnel* (New York: Knopf, 1990), in which a young girl searches through a frightening tunnel to find her brother; and *Changes* (New York: Knopf, 1992), about the effects of a new baby on an older brother (artistic style: surrealist/lifelike pictures)

copies of Ann Grifalconi's *Osa's Pride* (Boston: Little, Brown, 1990), which is set in Africa, about how the nurturing love of the grandmother helps Osa overcome her pride; and *The Village of Round and Small Houses* (Boston: Little, Brown, 1986), in which a grandmother tells the tale of why beyond the volcano, women live in round houses and men live in square houses (artistic style: vibrant pastels)

Activity

Explain that illustrators are people who draw and create the pictures seen in books and that sometimes they write the books as well. Make it clear that all illustrators have their own style or technique.

Read a book and follow up the reading by showing a transparency or picture from another book created by the same illustrator.

Encourage students to generate descriptive words that describe the illustrator's style.

Repeat this procedure for one or two more illustrators.

Have children then make an illustration modeled after their favorite illustrator.

Create a bulletin board or a class book with the children's pictures.

Books for Teaching About Illustrators for Grades K–6

Hutchins, Pat. *Rosie's Walk*. New York: Macmillan, 1968.   A rooster unknowingly sends a hen on a wild chase.

———. *Don't Forget the Bacon*. New York: Greenwillow, 1976.   A young boy is sent to get groceries by his mother and tries to remember the shopping list.
      (artistic style: lines and patterns to depict texture)

Sendak, Maurice. *Where the Wild Things Are*. New York: Harper and Row, 1963. A young boy named Max takes a dream trip to a far-off land of wild things.

———. *Chicken Soup with Rice*. New York: Harper and Row, 1962. Praises, songs, pictures, and hymns in honor of the months of the year accompany a tale about the author's favorite soup.
      (artistic style: fanciful watercolor figures)

5
Picture Storybooks

An Extraordinary Egg

Purpose

- To introduce children to picture story-books.

- To help children recognize characteristics of picture storybooks.

- To have children create an original picture storybook.

Materials

large pieces of construction paper with writing space at the bottom

crayons

pencils

large pictures of interesting scenes

copy of *An Extraordinary Egg* by Leo Lionni (New York: Knopf, 1994), in which three frogs befriend an alligator after mistaking it for a chicken.

Activity

 Show the large pictures to the class. Ask them to describe what is happening in each picture and to think of words to go along with the pictures.

Hang the pictures on the chalkboard and write their descriptions underneath.

Explain that books that contain pictures with matching words like the ones on the board are called picture storybooks.

Reinforce the idea that the book would not be complete without its illustrations.

Ask students to listen while you read a picture storybook to see if the words describe the pictures, and read the Lionni book.

Have each student draw a picture on a large piece of construction paper and write words or sentences to describe the picture.

Collect all the work and bind the pages into a class picture storybook.

Picture Storybooks for Grades K–2

Pfister, Marcus. *The Rainbow Fish.* New York: North-South Books, 1992. Rainbow Fish is the most beautiful fish in the entire ocean. However, his refusal to share his sparkling silver scales has made him the loneliest fish, until he learns to share and make friends.

Ross, Tom, and Rex Barron. *Eggbert, the Slightly Cracked Egg*. **New York: Putnam, 1994.**   Eggbert is very popular in the refrigerator, until it is discovered that he is slightly cracked and is sent away. On his journeys Eggbert comes to realize that our flaws are natural and something to be proud of.

Picture Storybooks for Grades 3–6

Bunting, Eve. *Smoky Night*. **New York: Harcourt Brace, 1994.**   A boy, his mother, and their cat are caught in the middle of the L.A. riots when their apartment is set on fire. These events bring them together with a family of a different race.

Schimmel, Schim. *Dear Children of the Earth: A Letter from Home*. **Minocqua, WI: NorthWord Press, 1994.**   A letter from Mother Earth asks the children of the world to help protect their brother and sister animals and the environment.

Van Allsburg, Chris. *Just a Dream*. **Boston: Houghton Mifflin, 1990.**   Walter is a litterbug. He never sorts his recyclables. One night his magic bed takes him into the future, where he discovers that the environment has been harmed. When Walter awakes, he rethinks his litterbug ways.

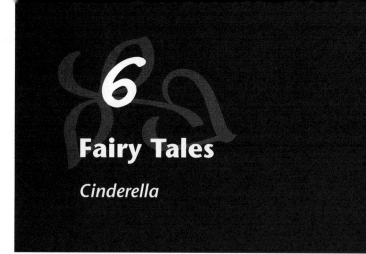

6

Fairy Tales

Cinderella

Purpose

To have students:

- Understand and identify characteristics of fairy tales.

- Retell fairy tales.

Materials

chart paper

markers

storytelling technique of choice: puppets, felt board, stick puppets, etc.

copy of *Cinderella* by Charles Perrault (New York: Scribner's, 1954)

Activity

Describe the characteristics of fairy tales: there are usually only a few characters; some of the characters are good and some are bad; usually something bad happens to the good character; there is some unreal element, such as a fairy, an elf, magic, etc.; the main character usually winds up happy at the end of the story.

Ask students to listen for these characteristics as you read the story of *Cinderella*. Then read the story.

Ask students to recall the fairy tale characteristics. List their responses on chart paper.

Retell the story in your own words using a storytelling technique (to model a fairy tale retelling).

Explain that after a few readings and practice, students will retell their own fairy tale to the class.

Fairy Tales for Grades K–2

Grimm, Jacob. *Snow White and the Seven Dwarfs*. Boston: Little, Brown, 1974. A princess left to die in the woods is cared for by seven little men.

Rika, Lesser. *Hansel and Gretel*. New York: Dodd, Mead, 1984. A poor woodcutter's children get lost in the forest. They find a candy house, but a wicked witch lives there and plans to eat them for supper.

Scieszka, Jon, and Lane Smith. *The Stinky Cheese Man and Other Fairly Stupid Tales*. New York: Viking, 1992.   Zany re-creations of familiar fairy tales.

Fairy Tales for Grades 3–6

Hodges, Margaret. *Saint George and the Dragon*. Boston: Little, Brown, 1984.   A knight slays a dragon who has been attacking a kingdom and brings happiness to the land.

Louie, Ai-Ling. *Yeh-Shen: A Cinderella Story from China*. New York: Philomel, 1982. A young Chinese girl struggles against her stepmother and stepsisters and becomes the bride of a prince.

Young, Ed. *Lon Po Po: A Red Riding Hood Story from China*. New York: Philomel, 1989.   Three sisters are left home alone and are threatened by a fierce and hungry wolf who is camouflaged as their grandmother.

7

Fables, Folktales, and Legends

The Tortoise and the Hare

Purpose

To have children:

- Understand, identify, and describe characteristics of a fables, folktales, and legends.

- Write an original fable, folktale, or legend.

Materials

stuffed animals: one turtle and one rabbit

piece of string (for finish line)

a rock

small tree-like plant

writing paper and pencils

copy of *More Fables of Aesop: The Tortoise and the Hare* by Jack Kent (New York: Parent's Magazine Press, 1974)

Activity

 Describe the characteristics of a fable: characters are usually animals or other non-humans; there are just a few characters; the story is simple and teaches a lesson.

 Tell the story *The Tortoise and the Hare* using props.

 Have children choose a partner to write a fable with. Have the partners work together in writing and illustrating an original fable. Encourage the teams to present their fable to the class. Be available to assist the children in writing their fables as needed. Do the same with folktales and legends.

Fables, Folktales, and Legends for Grades K–2

Lionni, Leo. *Frederick*. New York: Pantheon, 1967. While several field mice gather supplies for the upcoming winter, Frederick gathers something that is irreplaceable.

Lobel, Arnold. *Ming Lo Moves the Mountain.* New York: Greenwillow, 1982. Unhappy with a mountain being at the foot of their house, Ming Lo and his wife consult a wise man, who shows them how they can move their house.

Young, Ed. *Seven Blind Mice*. New York: Scholastic, 1995. Seven courageous mice set out to discover something that rests by the pond. Each mouse has his own opinion as to what it is.

Fables, Folktales, and Legends for Grades 3–6

Cooney, Barbara. *Chanticleer and the Fox*. New York: Thomas Crowell, 1958.   A clever fox tries to outsmart a proud rooster through the use of flattery.

Showalter, Jean B. *The Donkey Ride*. New York: Doubleday, 1967.   Retelling of Aesop's fable about a father and son who, while on their way to market, keep taking the advice of people they meet.

Steptoe, John. *The Story of Jumping Mouse: Native American Legend*. New York: Lothrop, Lee and Shepard, 1984.   A little mouse sets out to see the world and learns a great many things.

8
Realistic Literature

Tight Times

Purpose

- To introduce realistic literature to children.
- To help children recognize characteristics of realistic literature.
- To have children create an original realistic story.

Materials

large pieces of construction paper

pencils

markers

chart paper

copy of *Tight Times* by Barbara Shook Hazen (New York: Viking, 1979), about a youngster who isn't sure why a thing called "tight times" means not getting a dog

Activity

 Explain that realistic literature consists of stories about something that could actually happen in real life. They are about serious topics and how to deal with them.

 Read the story *Tight Times*.

Ask children to identify the parts of the story that could really happen. Discuss those events.

During a shared writing activity, write a realistic story on chart paper about something that could happen to the whole class, such as going on a class trip and losing a member of the class while on the trip.

Have students work independently to construct a short creative writing piece that describes a realistic problem they had in their life.

Have them illustrate their stories.

Realistic Literature for Grades K–2

Alexander, Martha. *Nobody Asked Me If I Wanted a Baby Sister.* New York: Dial, 1971. Resenting the attention and praise lavished on his new baby sister, Oliver tries to give her away to his neighbors.

Lapsley, S. *I Am Adopted*. New York: Bradbury, 1975.   A little boy explains what it means to be adopted.

Wolf, Bernard. *Don't Feel Sorry for Paul*. Philadelphia: Lippincott, 1974.   Two weeks in the life of a handicapped boy as he learns to live successfully in a world made for people without handicaps.

Realistic Literature for Grades 3–6

Durant, Penny Raife. *When Heroes Die*. New York: Aladdin, 1994.   Twelve-year-old Gary needs advice and guidance when he finds out that his Uncle Rob, his hero, is dying of AIDS. Uncle Rob himself is the one who gives Gary strength to face the future.

Sobol, Harriet Langsam. *My Brother Steven is Retarded*. New York: Macmillan, 1977. An eleven-year-old girl talks about the mixed feelings she has for her older, mentally retarded brother.

———. *My Other-Mother, My Other-Father*. New York: Macmillan, 1979.   Twelve-year-old Andrea, whose parents are divorced and remarried, discusses the problems and joys of being part of a new, larger family.

9 Biography

If You Grew Up with George Washington

Purpose

- To introduce children to biographies.
- To help children recognize characteristics of a biography.
- To have children write an original biography.

Materials

writing paper

pencils

crayons

book-binding materials

pictures of each student

copy of *If You Grew Up with George Washington* by Ruth Gross (New York: Scholastic, 1982)

Activity

Ask children to name some famous people they would like to learn about and how they would go about finding information about them (TV, books, newspapers).

Explain that biographies tell us the story of someone's life.

Tell students that the author of a biography is not the actual person the book is about, just as Ruth Gross is the author of a book about George Washington.

Ask students to listen to or read the biography *If You Grew Up with George Washington* so that they will be able to discuss the facts about his life.

Have each child write a biography about someone in the class. Pair off the children and allow them to interview each other about their life histories: where they were born, where they live, their family, friends, and hobbies. Be sure each child takes notes.

Have children illustrate the pages of their biography; use the photographs of each child in the published bound books.

Biographies for Grades K–2

Aliki. *The Many Lives of Benjamin Franklin*. Englewood Cliffs, NJ: Prentice Hall, 1977.

Austin, James. Easy to Read Discovery Books. Champaign, IL: Garrard, 1960. Series includes biographies of Daniel Boone, Lafayette, Theodore Roosevelt, Abraham Lincoln, George Washington Carver, Clara Barton, Paul Revere, and the Wright Brothers.

Sutton, Felix. *Master of Ballyhoo: The Story of P. T. Barnum*. New York: Putnam, 1968.

Biographies for Grades 3–6

Brown, Gene. *Anne Frank: Child of the Holocaust*. New York: Blackbirch, 1991.

Daugherty, James. *Daniel Boone*. New York: Viking, 1966.

Mitchell, Barbara. *A Pocketful of Goobers: A Story About George Washington Carver*. Minneapolis: Carolrhoda Books, 1986.

10

Poetry

Blackberry Ink

Purpose

- To introduce children to poetry.
- To have children write and illustrate an original poem.

Materials

chart paper

markers

pencils

crayons

copy of *Blackberry Ink* by Eve Merriam (New York: William Morrow, 1985)

Activity

Recite a few poems (such as "Humpty Dumpty") to children.

Ask them what we call things that sound like that (Poems).

Ask what makes them poems (Rhyme or other sounds that are similar to each other, rather short length, one topic each).

Read poems from *Blackberry Ink*.

Encourage children who know poems to recite them.

Ask children to write a poem together. Write the word "snow" in the middle of the chart paper. Ask children what snow is like, and how it looks and feels. Write their responses to the left of the word "snow." For example:

What is it like?	Who or what?
white	snow
bright	
wet	
cold	
fluffy	

Chant each pair of words together (white snow, bright snow, wet snow, etc.). Then ask children what snow does, and write their responses to the right of the word "snow." For example:

What is it like?	Who or what?	What does it do?
white	snow	blows
bright		drifts
wet		flurries
cold		melts

Chant the poem in rhyme:

White snow blows,

Bright snow drifts,

Wet snow flurries,

Cold snow melts.

 Have children write their own poems using the three questions (1) Who or what? (2) What is it like? (3) What does it do?

 Share the poems with the class and bind them into a class book.

Poetry for Grades K–2

Goldstein, Bobbye S. *What's on the Menu?* New York: Viking, 1992.

———. *Inner Chimes*. Honesdale, PA: Boyds Mills Press, 1994.

———. *Special Times*. New York: Bantam, 1994.

Poetry for Grades 3–6

Hudson, Wade. *Pass It on: African American Poetry for Children*. New York: Scholastic, 1993.

Prelutsky, Jack. *It's Thanksgiving*. New York: Scholastic, 1982.

Silverstein, Shel. *Where the Sidewalk Ends*. New York: Harper and Row, 1974.

———. *A Light in the Attic*. New York: Harper and Row, 1981.

———. *Falling Up*. New York: HarperCollins, 1996.

Part 4

Becoming Successful Writers

This section is meant to provide teachers of grades K–6 with ways to introduce the writing process and promote daily voluntary writing. Students work through each step of the writing process: prewriting or brainstorming, composing first drafts, engaging in peer and teacher conferences, editing, illustrating, and publishing original stories that express their ideas, feelings, hopes, and dreams. All students are given the opportunity to discuss their works in progress and present their published books. Storytelling techniques can be used as children retell their original stories. Each child's book should include a comment page at the end where other students may write positive remarks.

Introduction to Journal Writing

Purpose

To have children:

- Engage in the roles of author and illustrator.
- Improve on their existing writing abilities.

Materials

notebook

pencils

crayons

Activity

Explain that everyone has the ability to be a reader, a writer, and an illustrator. Let students know that one way to do this is to keep a journal. Tell students that many authors and illustrators get ideas through their own journals.

Explain that a journal is a special and personal place to record daily thoughts, feelings, and ideas in both written and illustrative form.

Show children how journal pages are dated.

Set aside allocated time for daily journal writing.

Allow time for students to share journal entries with the class.

Encourage children to personalize their journal by decorating the cover.

2
Creating Original Stories

Purpose

- To teach children the elements of a well-formed story.

- To help children increase their oral language and writing abilities.

- To have children create and present original stories through active storytelling.

Materials

felt board characters

popsicle stick figures

hand puppets

See Lessons 1 and 3 in Part 2, "Storytelling Techniques," for guidelines on making felt board characters and puppets.

Activity

 After introducing students to the concept of storytelling using the felt board, popsicle stick puppets, and hand puppets, retell a familiar story using one of these techniques. At the completion of the story, ask students questions that identify story elements:

Where did the story take place?

Who were the main characters?

What was the problem and how was it solved?

Have students identify each story element and ask them to include them in stories of their own.

Have children pick their favorite part of their own story and create appropriate character props for use in a presentation of their story.

3 Writing Stories and Making Bound Books

Purpose

- To introduce children to the publishing process.
- To have children write a rough draft of a story of their own.

Materials

writing paper

copies of books by various authors

materials for making bound books (see pages 210–212)

Activity

Explain that each author has his or her own writing style. Read excerpts from several books to illustrate different writing styles.

Talk with children about writing their own books with their own individual style.

Have students write rough drafts of an original story.

Teach children how to make their own bound books. Directions for making books for children's own stories, special class books on certain themes, and Big Books follow. Children in grades 3–6 are usually capable of making their own books; children in grades K–2 usually need assistance.

Making Bound Books

After writing an original story, a child can illustrate and publish his or her own book. This book can be placed in the classroom library. The following are directions for one method that a child can follow to make such a book. (Dimensions can be adjusted to make larger or smaller books.)

Directions:

1. Place 11" x 14" (27.5 cm x 35 cm) pieces of wallpaper (or plastic or cloth) face down. Paste two pieces of 6" x 9" (15 cm x 22.5 cm) oaktag or cardboard on the wallpaper 1/4" (0.5 cm) apart, leaving about a 1" (2.5 cm) border.
2. Fold each corner of the wallpaper from the corner points onto the cardboard to form a triangle; paste down. Fold flaps onto the cardboard and paste.
3. Next, using a large needle and strong thread, sew a running stitch down the center of 10 or more sheets of 8 1/2" x 11" (21 cm x 27.5 cm) plain white paper. Fold along the stitched line.
4. Put glue on the 1/4" (0.5 cm) space between the pieces of cardboard and also on the entire exposed area of the cardboard. Place the folded and stitched edge of the plain paper in the 1/4" (0.5 cm) glued space; paste the first and last sheets onto the cardboard and over the wallpaper border to make the inside covers.
5. Add a design to the finished cover.

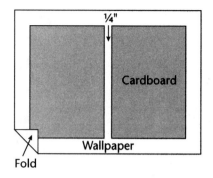

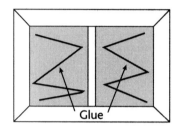

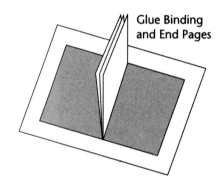

Class-Made Books

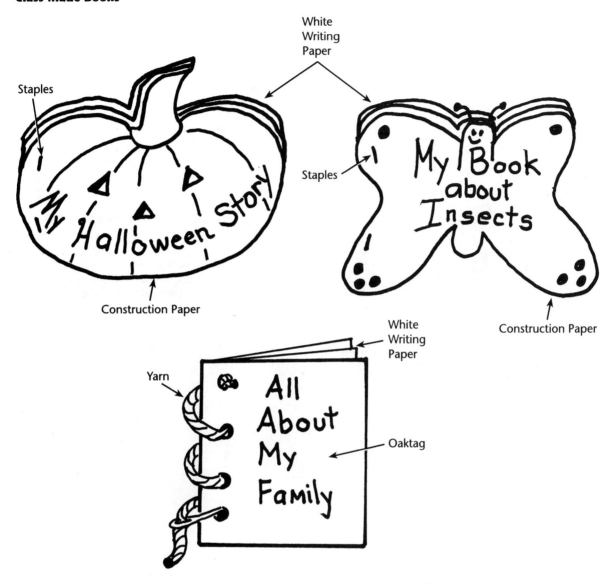

For special class themes or for children's own books, other types of bound books can be created.

Stapled Book
A stapled book can be made by cutting colored construction paper and white writing paper into a desired shape, and then stapling at the side.

Sewn Book
A simple sewn book can be made by punching holes into oaktag and white writing paper, and then sewing the pages together with yarn.

Making Big Books

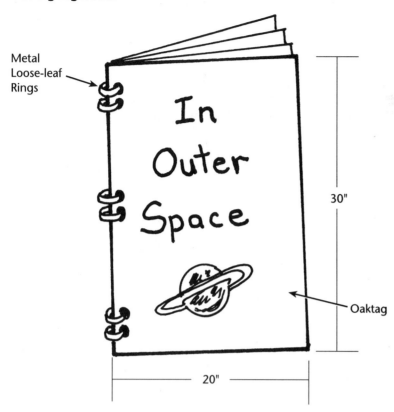

Metal
Loose-leaf
Rings

*In
Outer
Space*

30"

Oaktag

20"

Materials
12 pieces of oaktag (20" x 30")
6 loose-leaf rings (1 1/4")
Hole punch

Directions:
Punch three sets of holes in the top, middle, and bottom of the oaktag as shown in the diagram. Insert a loose-leaf ring in each hole. The Big Book should be a minimum of ten pages or as many as is manageable. The print should be 1 1/2" to 2" high.

4

Writing Series Books

Purpose

• To introduce children to series books.

• To have children write sequels to existing books.

Materials

writing paper

pencils

publishing materials

Activity

Discuss how authors may write different stories for the same characters.

Discuss similarities in style and illustrations within a series.

Talk about how readers who enjoy one book in a series often like others from that series as well.

Have students choose a favorite author's latest book in a series and write a new story for that series, following the same writing and illustrative style (see Lesson 3 in Part 3 on series books).

5

Writing a Science Story

Purpose

To show children how to use factual information and reference books to write and illustrate an original science story.

Materials

writing paper

pencils

reference books: dictionary, encyclopedia, science magazines, science books

copy of *A Seed Is a Promise* by Claire Merril (New York: Scholastic, 1990)

Activity

Create a "KWL" chart about plants: *K* for answers to the question "What do we *know* about the topic?", *W* for "*What* do we want to learn about the topic?", and *L* for "What did we *learn* about the topic?"

Brainstorm to fill in the *K* and *W* sections of the chart. Read and discuss *A Seed Is a Promise* and complete the *L* section.

Have students write original science stories about plants using information gathered on the KWL chart or from additional independent research gathered from available reference materials and science books. Encourage them to include as many facts and new words as possible.

Part 5

Special Events

The activities in this section celebrate literature through parent, school, and local community involvement. These activities will help foster children's appreciation of literacy, promote voluntary reading and writing, and encourage pride in achievement.

Everyone Reads Day

Purpose

- To have students create invitations and (later) thank-you cards for guest readers.

- To demonstrate that everyone in the school building is interested in books.

Preparation

Recruit various adults in the children's lives (the principal, the school nurse, the secretaries, the custodians, the aides, parents) to visit the classroom as guest readers.

Materials

materials for invitations and thank-you cards

appropriate stories to be read to children by guest readers

Activity

Have students work in small groups to write and illustrate invitations for Everyone Reads Day; make sure essential information (day, time, and place) is included.

Invite participants to read to small groups of children. Ask guests to select stories they want to read. Allow them to choose books from a preapproved literature list, from the bookshelf, or one of their own books.

Have each guest read to three or four children at a time.

Have children move in the same groups to each guest reader until they have heard around four different stories.

Afterward, have students construct cards to thank the guest readers for their contributions and invite them to come again.

2

Trip to the Public Library

Purpose

To introduce children to the public library.

Preparation

Make arrangements with library personnel for the class visit.

Recruit family volunteers to accompany the group.

Arrange transportation.

Remind children to bring their library cards, if they have them.

Activity

Explain that the class will be going to the public library to see the books and to learn how the library works.

Review the rules for library behavior: speak quietly, handle books carefully, return a book to its proper place on the shelf.

Once at the library, ask the librarian to lead the tour, talk about the library, explain the card catalog or computerized catalog, read to the children, and discuss how the children may borrow books.

Let children select books. Help those who do not already have library cards obtain them.

3

Trip to the Bookstore

Purpose

To introduce children to a bookstore.

Preparation

Make arrangements with the bookstore personnel for the class visit.

Recruit family volunteers to accompany the group.

Arrange transportation.

Activity

Explain to the class that you will be going to a bookstore where there will be thousands of books.

Review rules they must follow: handle books with care, speak quietly, place books exactly where they found them.

Travel to the bookstore and take a tour.

Spend time in the children's section and point out familiar authors, illustrators, and books.

Return to the classroom and share thoughts on the experience.

Allow children to show the class any books they purchased.

4

Book Celebration Day

Purpose

• To celebrate books and children's accomplishments with reading.

• To use and display the methods, techniques, and materials used as part of the literacy program.

Materials

costumes representing book characters

books

roll movies

felt board stories

puppets

other items that illustrate characters or stories from favorite books

Activity

Tell children that the class will be having a Book Celebration Day. Explain that it is a day to celebrate books and share the good times they have had with books.

Help students decide what activities they might do on this special day. Some possibilities include:

Dress up as a book character.

Read a book to the class.

Retell a story using a storytelling technique of their choice.

Remind children to prepare in advance. Note what you, the teacher, will need to supply or contribute to each child's presentation or activity.

Be sure each child has at least one opportunity to share and contribute to the festivities.

Afterward, review and discuss the day.

Bibliography

Professional Literature

Anderson, R. C., L. G. Fielding, and P. T. Wilson. 1988. Growth in Reading and How Children Spend Their Time Outside of School. *Reading Research Quarterly* 23: 285–303.

Anderson, R. C., E. H. Hiebert, J. A. Scott, and I. A. G. Wilkinson. 1985. *Becoming a Nation of Readers: The Report of the Commission on Reading.* Washington, DC: National Institute of Education.

Applebee, A. N., J. A. Langer, and M. Mullis. 1988. *Who Reads Best? Factors Related to Reading Achievement in Grades 3, 7, and 11.* Princeton, NJ: Educational Testing Service.

Arbuthnot, M. H., and Z. Sutherland. 1977. *Children and Books.* 5th ed. Glenview, IL: Scott, Foresman.

Atwell, N. 1987. *In the Middle.* Portsmouth, NH: Heinemann.

Augustine, D., K. Gruber, and L. Hanson. 1989. Cooperation Works. *Educational Leadership* 4–7.

Beckman, D. 1972. Interior Space: The Things of Education. *National Elementary Principal* 52: 43–49.

Bergeron, B. 1990. What Does the Term Whole Language Mean? A Definition from the Literature. *Journal of Reading Behavior* 23: 301–29.

Bissett, D. 1970. The Usefulness of Children's Books in the Reading Program. In J. Catterson, ed., *Children and Literature.* Newark, DE: International Reading Association.

Bissex, G. 1980. *GNYS at Work: A Child Learns to Write and Read.* Cambridge, MA: Harvard University Press.

Bloom, B. 1964. *Stability and Change in Human Characteristics.* New York: John Wiley.

Boorstin, D. 1984. Letter of Transmittal. In *Books in Our Future: A Report from the Librarian of Congress to the Congress.* Washington, DC: U.S. Congress, Joint Committee on the Library.

Bossert, S. T. 1979. *Tasks and Social Relationships in Classrooms.* Cambridge, UK: Cambridge University Press.

Calkins, L. M. 1986. *The Art of Teaching Writing.* Portsmouth, NH: Heinemann.

Cazden, C. 1986. Classroom Discourse. In M. C. Wittrock, ed., *The Handbook of Research on Teaching,* 3rd ed., pp. 432–63. New York: Macmillan.

Clay, M. 1976. Early Childhood and Cultural Diversity in New Zealand. *Reading Teacher* 29: 333–42.

Cohen, D. A. 1968. The Effects of Literacy on Vocabulary and Reading Achievements. *Elementary English* 45: 209–13, 217.

Cullinan, B. E., ed. 1987. *Children's Literature in the Reading Program.* Newark, DE: International Reading Association.

———. 1992. *Invitation to Read: More Children's Literature in the Reading Program.* Newark, DE: International Reading Association.

Cunningham, A. E., and K. E. Stanovich. 1991. Tracking the Unique Effects of Print Exposure in Children: Associations with Vocabulary, General Knowledge, and Spelling. *Journal of Educational Psychology* 83: 264–74.

Daniels, H. 1994. *Literature Circles: Voice and Choice in the Student-Centered Classroom.* York, ME: Stenhouse.

Dewey, J. 1966. *Democracy and Education.* New York: Free Press. (Original work published 1916.)

Durkin, D. 1966. *Children Who Read Early.* New York: Teachers College Press.

Feitleson, D., B. Kita, and Z. Goldstein. 1986. Effects of Listening to Series of Stories on First Graders' Comprehension and Use of Language. *Journal of Research and the Teaching of English* 20: 339–56.

Field, T. 1980. Preschool Play: Effects of Teacher/Child Ratios and Organization of Classroom Space. *Child Study Journal* 10: 191–205.

Ford, M. E. 1992. *Motivating Humans: Goals, Emotions and Personal Agency Beliefs.* Newbury Park, CA: Sage.

Forman, E., and C. Cazden. 1985. Exploring Vygotskian Perspectives in Education: The Cognitive Value of Peer Interaction. In J. Wertsch, ed., *Culture, Communication, and Cognition: Vygotskian Perspectives,* pp. 323–47. Cambridge, UK: Cambridge University Press.

Golub, J., ed. 1988. *Focus on Collaborative Learning*. Urbana, IL: National Council of Teachers of English.

Goodman, K. S. 1989a. Whole-Language Research: Foundations of Development. *Elementary School Journal* 90: 207–20.

———. 1989b. Roots of the Whole Language Movement. *Elementary School Journal* 90: 113–27.

Graves, D. H. 1975. An Examination of the Writing Process of Seven-Year-Old Children. *Research in the Teaching of English* 9: 227–41.

———. 1983. *Writing: Teachers and Children at Work*. Portsmouth, NH: Heinemann.

Greaney, V. 1980. Factors Related to Amount and Type of Leisure Time Reading. *Reading Research Quarterly* 15: 337–57.

Greaney, V., and M. Hegarty. 1987. Correlates of Leisure Time Reading. *Journal of Research in Reading* 10: 3–20.

Gundlack, R., J. McLane, F. Scott, and G. McNamee. 1985. The Social Foundations of Early Writing Development. In M. Farr, ed., *Advances in Writing Research: Vol 1. Children's Early Writing Development*. Norwood, NJ: Ablex.

Guthrie, J. T., and V. Greaney. 1991. Literacy Acts. In R. Barr, M. L. Kamil, P. Mosenthal, and P. D. Pierson, eds., *Handbook of Reading Research* 2: 68–96. New York: Longman.

Hansen, J. S. 1969. The Impact of the Home Literacy Environment on Reading Attitude. *Elementary English* 46: 17–24.

Hoffman, J. V., N. L. Roser, and C. Farest. 1988. Literature Sharing Strategies in Classrooms Serving Students from Economically Disadvantaged and Language Different Home Environments. In J. E. Readance and R. S. Baldwin, eds., *Dialogues in Literacy Research: Thirty-Seventh Yearbook of the National Reading Conference*. Chicago: National Reading Conference.

Holdaway, D. 1979. *The Foundations of Literacy*. Sydney: Ashton Scholastic.

Huck, C. 1976. *Children's Literature in the Elementary School*. 3rd ed. New York: Holt.

Ingham, J. 1981. *Books and Reading Development*. London: Heinemann.

Irving, A. 1980. *Promoting Voluntary Reading for Children and Young People*. Paris: UNESCO.

Irwin, P. A., and J. N. Mitchell. 1983. A Procedure for Assessing the Richness of Retellings. *Journal of Reading* 26: 391–96.

Johnson, D. W., and R. T. Johnson. 1987. *Learning Together and Alone: Cooperative, Competitive, and Individualistic Learning*. 2nd ed. Englewood Cliffs, NJ: Prentice Hall.

Johnson, D. W., G. Maruyama, R. Johnson, D. Nelson, and L. Skon. 1981. Effects of Cooperative, Competitive, and Individualistic Goal Structures on Achievement: A Meta-Analysis. *Psychological Bulletin* 89: 47–62.

Johnson, N. O. 1995. Four Second-Grade Children's Responses to Literature. Ph.D. diss., Rutgers University, New Brunswick, NJ.

Kagan, S., G. L. Zahn, K. F. Widaman, J. Schwarzwald, and G. Tyrell. 1985. Classroom Structural Bias: Impact of Cooperative and Competitive Individuals and Groups. In R. Slavin, S. Sharan, S. Kagan, R. Hertz Lazarovitz, C. Webb, and R. Schmuck, eds., *Learning to Cooperate, Cooperating to Learn*, pp. 277–312. New York: Plenum.

Kritchevsky, S., and E. Prescott. 1977. *Planning Environment for Young Children: Physical Space*. Washington, DC: National Association for the Education of Young Children.

Lamme, L. L., and L. Ledbetter. 1990. Libraries: The Heart of Whole Language. *Language Arts* 67: 735–41.

Lew, M., D. Mesch, D. W. Johnson, and R. Johnson. 1986. Positive Interdependence, Academic and Collaborative Skills Group Contigencies, and Isolated Students. *American Educational Research Journal* 23: 476–88.

Lomax, L. M. 1976. Interest in Books and Stories at Nursery School. *Educational Research* 19: 100–112.

Loughlin, C. E., and M. D. Martin. 1987. *Supporting Literacy: Developing Effective Learning Environments*. New York: Teachers College Press.

Mandler, J., and N. Johnson. 1977. Remembrance of Things Parsed: Story Structure and Recall. *Cognitive Psychology* 9: 111–51.

McCombs, B. L. 1991. Unraveling Motivation: New Perspectives from Research and Practice. *Journal of Experimental Education* 60: 3–88.

McConaughy, S. 1980. Using Story Structure in the Classroom. *Language Arts* 57: 157–64.

Montessori, M. 1965. *Spontaneous Activity in Education*. New York: Schocken.

Moon, C., and G. Wells. 1979. The Influence of Home on Learning to Read. *Journal of Research and Reading* 2: 53–62.

Moore, G. 1986. Effects of the Spatial Definition of Behavior Setting on Children's Behavior: A Quasi-Experimental Field Study. *Journal of Environmental Psychology* 6: 205–31.

Morrison, G. S. 1988. *Early Childhood Education Today*. 4th ed. Columbus, OH: Merrill.

Morrow, L. M. 1982. Relationships Between Literature Programs, Library Corner, Designs and Children's Use of Literature. *Journal of Educational Research* 75: 339–44.

———. 1983. Home and School Correlates of Early Interest in Literature. *Journal of Educational Research* 76: 221–30.

———. 1988. Young Children's Responses to One-to-One Story Readings in School Settings. *Reading Research Quarterly* 27: 250–75.

———. 1990. The Impact of Classroom Environmental Changes on the Promotion of Literacy During Play. *Early Childhood Research Quarterly* 5: 537–54.

———. 1992. The Impact of a Literature-Based Program on Literacy Achievement, Use of Literature, and Attitudes of Children from Minority Backgrounds. *Reading Research Quarterly* 27: 250–75.

———. 1996. Motivating Reading and Writing in Diverse Classrooms: Social and Physical Context in a Literature-Based Program. *National Council of Teachers of English Research Report 28*. Urbana, IL: National Council of Teachers of English.

———. 1997. *Literacy Development in the Early Years: Helping Children Read and Write*. 3rd ed. Boston: Allyn and Bacon.

Morrow, L. M., E. O'Connor, and J. K. Smith. 1990. Effects of a Story Reading Program on the Literacy Development of At-Risk Kindergarten Children. *Journal of Reading Behavior* 22: 225–75.

Morrow, L. M., and M. K. Rand. 1991. Preparing the Classroom Physical Environment to Promote Literacy Behavior During Play: Implications from Research. In J. Christie, ed., *Play and Literacy Development*. New York: SUNY Press.

Morrow, L. M., and C. S. Weinstein. 1982. Increasing Children's Use of Literature Through Program and Physical Design Changes. *Elementary School Journal* 83: 131–97.

———. 1986. Encouraging Voluntary Reading: The Impact of a Literature Program on Children's Use of Library Centers. *Reading Research Quarterly* 21: 330–46.

Nash, B. 1981. The Effects of Classroom Spatial Organization on Four- and Five-Year-Old Children's Learning. *British Journal of Educational Psychology* 51: 144–55.

National Reading Research Center. 1991. Conceptual Framework: The Engagement Perspective. In *National Reading Research Center: A Proposal from the University of Maryland and the University of Georgia*. Athens, GA, and College Park, MD: National Reading Research Center.

Neuman, S., and K. Roskos. 1990. The Influence of Literacy-Enriched Play Settings on Preschoolers' Engagement with Written Language. In J. Zutell and S. McCormick, eds., *Literacy Theory and Research: Analysis from Multiple Paradigms*, pp. 179–87. Thirty-ninth Yearbook of the National Reading Conference. Chicago: National Reading Conference.

———. 1992. Literacy Objects as Cultural Tools: Effects on Children's Literacy Behaviors in Play. *Reading Research Quarterly* 27: 203–25.

Newman, J., ed. 1985. *Whole Language: Theory in Use*. Portsmouth, NH: Heinemann.

O'Flahavan, J., L. B. Gambrell, J. Gutherie, S. Stahal, J. F. Baumann, and D. E. Aluermann. 1992. Poll Results Guide Activities of Research Center. *Reading Today* 10 (1): 12.

Pappas, C., B. Kiefer, and L. Levstik. 1990. *An Integrated Language Perspective in the Elementary School: Theory into Action*. New York: Longman.

Pellegrini, A., and L. Galda. 1982. The Effects of Thematic Fantasy Play Training on the Development of Children's Story Comprehension. *American Educational Research Journal* 19: 443–52.

Piaget, J. 1959. *The Language and Thought of the Child*. 3rd ed. London: Routledge and Kegan Paul.

Piaget, J., and B. Inhelder. 1969. *Psychology of the Child*. New York: Basic Books.

Rand, M. 1994. Using Thematic Instruction to Organize an Integrated Language Arts Classroom. In L. M. Morrow, J. K. Smith, and L. C. Wilkinson, eds., *Integrated Language Arts: Controversy to Consensus*. Boston, MA: Allyn and Bacon.

Rivlin, L., and C. S. Weinstein. 1984. Educational Issues, School Settings, and Environmental Psychology. *Journal of Environmental Psychology* 4: 347–64.

Routman, R. 1991. *Invitations: Changing as Teachers and Learners, K-12*. Portsmouth, NH: Heinemann.

Sakamoto, T., and M. Makita. 1973. Japan. In J. Downing, ed., *Comparative Reading*. New York: Macmillan.

Saltz, E., and J. Johnson. 1974. Training for the Thematic-Fantasy Play in Culturally Disadvantaged Children. Preliminary Results. *Journal of Educational Psychology* 66: 623–30.

Schickedanz, J. A. 1993. Designing the Early Childhood Classroom Environment to Facilitate Literacy Development. In B. Spodack and A. Sarancho, eds., *Language and Literacy in Early Childhood Education: Yearbook in Early Childhood*

Education. Vol. 4. New York: Teachers College Press.

Sharan, Y., and S. Sharan. 1989–90. Group Investigation Expands Cooperative Learning. *Educational Leadership* 47: 17–21.

Sharkey, E. A. 1992. The Literacy Behaviors and Social Interactions of Children During an Independent Reading and Writing Period: An Ethnographic Study. Ph.D. diss., Rutgers University, New Brunswick, NJ.

Sirotnik, K. A. 1983. What You See Is What You Get: Consistency, Persistency, and Mediocracy in Classrooms. *Harvard Educational Review* 53: 16–31.

Slavin, R. E. 1983. Non-Cognitive Outcomes. In J. M. Levine and M. C. Wang, eds., *Teacher and Student Perceptions: Implications for Learning*. Hillsdale, NJ: Erlbaum.

———. 1985. An Introduction to Cooperative Learning Research. In R. Slavin, S. Sharan, S. Kagan, R. Hertz Lazarovitz, C. Webb, and R. Schmuck, eds., *Learning to Cooperate, Cooperating to Learn*, pp. 5–15. New York: Plenum.

———. 1990. *Cooperative Learning: Theory, Research, and Practice*. Englewood Cliffs, NJ: Prentice Hall.

Spaulding, C. I. 1992. The Motivation to Read and Write. In J. W. Irwin and M. A. Doyle, eds., *Reading/Writing Connections: Learning from Research*, pp. 177–201. Newark, DE: International Reading Association.

Spiegel, D. L. 1981. *Reading for Pleasure: Guidelines*. Newark, DE: International Reading Association.

Spivak, M. 1973. Archetypal Place. *Architectual Forum* 40: 40–44.

Stauffer, R. G. 1970. A Reading Teacher's Dream Come True. *Wilson Library Bulletin* 45: 282–92.

Stewig, J. W., and S. Sebesta, eds. 1978. *Using Literature in the Elementary Classroom*. Urbana, IL: National Council of Teachers of English.

Strickland, D. S., and D. Taylor. 1989. *Family Storybook Reading*. Portsmouth, NH: Heinemann.

Sutfin, H. 1980. The Effects on Children's Behavior of a Change in the Physical Design of a Kindergarten Classroom. Ph.D. diss., Boston University, Boston, MA.

Taylor, B. M., B. J. Frye, and M. Maruyama. 1990. Time Spent Reading and Reading Growth. *American Educational Research Journal* 27: 351–62.

Taylor, D. 1983. *Family Literacy*. Portsmouth, NH: Heinemann.

Teale, W. 1978. Positive Environments for Learning to Read: What Studies of Early Readers Tell Us. *Language Arts* 55: 922–32.

———. 1986. The Beginning of Reading and Writing: Written Language Development During the Preschool and Kindergarten Years. In M. Sampson, ed., *The Pursuit of Literacy: Early Reading and Writing*. Dubuque, IA: Kendal/Hunt.

Thorndyke, R. 1977. Cognitive Structures in Comprehension and Memory of Narrative Discourse. *Cognitive Psychology* 9: 77–110.

Vygotsky, L. S. 1978. *Mind and Society: The Development of Higher Psychological Processes*. Cambridge, MA: Harvard University Press.

Wells, C. G. 1985. *Language and Development in the Preschool Years*. Cambridge, UK: Cambridge University Press.

Wertsch, J. V. 1985. Adult-Child Interaction as a Source of Self-Regulation in Children. In S. Yussen, ed., *The Growth of Reflection in Children*. Orlando, FL: Academic Press.

Wood, K. 1990. Collaborative Learning. *Reading Teacher* 43: 346–47.

Yaden, D. 1985. Preschoolers' Spontaneous Inquiries About Print and Books. Paper presented at the annual meeting of the National Reading Conference, San Diego.

Children's Literature

Aardema, V. 1975. *Why Mosquitos Buzz in People's Ears*. New York: Dutton.

———. 1981. *Bringing the Rains to Kapiti Plain*. New York: Dial.

Arno, E. 1970. *The Gingerbread Man*. New York: Scholastic.

Asbojornsen, P. C., and E. M. Jorgen. 1957. *The Three Billy Goats Gruff*. New York: Harcourt Brace.

Babbitt, N. 1975. *Tuck Everlasting*. New York: HarperCollins.

Baker, L. 1990. *Life in the Rain Forests*. New York: Puffin.

Barrett, J. 1977. *Animals Should Definitely Not Wear Clothing*. New York: Aladdin.

———. 1978. *Cloudy with a Chance of Meatballs*. New York: Atheneum.

Bemelmans, L. 1977. *Madeline*. New York: Puffin.

Berger, M. 1992. *All About Seeds*. New York: Scholastic.

Bourgeois, P. 1986. *Franklin in the Dark*. New York: Scholastic.

Branley, F. 1985. *Volcanoes*. New York: Harper and Row.

Brenner, B. 1972. *The Three Little Pigs*. New York: Random House.

Brett, J. 1989. *The Mitten*. New York: Scholastic.

Brown, M. 1947. *Stone Soup*. New York: Scribner's.

———. 1957. *The Three Billy Goats Gruff*. New York: Harcourt Brace.

———. 1979. *Arthur's Eyes*. New York: Avon.

Buller, J., and S. Schade. 1988. *Space Rock*. New York: Random House.

Byron, B. 1981. *Wheels*. New York: Thomas Y. Crowell.

Carle, E. 1968. *One, Two, Three, to the Zoo*. New York: Philomel.

———. 1970. *The Very Hungry Caterpillar*. New York: Puffin.

———. 1983. *The Very Busy Spider*. New York: Philomel.

———. 1986. *The Grouchy Ladybug*. New York: HarperCollins.

Catling, P. S. 1979. *The Chocolate Touch*. New York: William Morrow.

Charles, F. 1951. *Jean Marie Counts Her Sheep*. New York: Scribner's.

Coerr, E. 1977. *Sadako and the Thousand Paper Cranes*. New York: Putnam.

Cole, J. 1987. *The Magic School Bus Inside the Earth*. New York: Scholastic.

———. 1990. *The Magic School Bus Lost in the Solar System*. New York: Scholastic.

Dahl, R. 1988. *James and the Giant Peach*. New York: Puffin.

Davidson, M. 1971. *Helen Keller*. New York: Hastings House.

de Paola, T. 1975. *Strega Nona*. Englewood Cliffs, NJ: Prentice Hall.

———. 1983. *The Legend of the Bluebonnet: An Old Tale of Texas*. New York: Putnam.

———. 1988. *The Legend of the Indian Paintbrush*. New York: Putnam.

Dorros, A. 1990. *Rain Forest Secrets*. New York: Scholastic.

Eastman, P. D. 1960. *Are You My Mother?* New York: Random House.

Flack, M. 1971. *Ask Mr. Bear*. New York: Macmillan.

Fleming, D. 1992. *Count!* New York: Scribner's.

Florian, D. 1986. *Discovering Trees*. New York: Scribner's.

Fujikawa, G. 1975. *Let's Eat*. New York: Grosset and Dunlap.

———. 1980. *Jenny Learns a Lesson*. New York: Grosset and Dunlap.

Galdone, P. 1972. *Goldilocks and the Three Bears*. New York: Seabury.

———. 1975a. *The Gingerbread Boy*. New York: Seabury.

———. 1975b. *The Little Red Hen*. New York: Scholastic.

George, J. C. 1959. *My Side of the Mountain*. New York: Dutton.

Gerstein, M. 1987. *The Mountains of Tibet*. New York: Harper and Row.

Grimm Brothers. 1968. *Little Red Riding Hood*. New York: Harcourt Brace.

Hoban, R. 1964. *Bread and Jam for Frances*. New York: Harper and Row.

Hodges, M. 1984. *Saint George and the Dragon: A Golden Legend*. Boston: Little, Brown.

Johnson, C. 1955. *Harold and the Purple Crayon*. New York: Harper and Row.

Kasza, K. 1988. *The Pig's Picnic*. New York: Putnam.

Keats, E. J. 1962. *The Snowy Day*. New York: Viking.

———. 1966. *Jenny's Hat*. New York: Harper and Row.

———. 1967. *Peter's Chair*. New York: Harper and Row.

———. 1968. *A Letter to Amy*. New York: Harper and Row.

———. 1972. *The Pet Show*. New York: Macmillan.

Kessler, L. P. 1966. *Kick, Pass, and Run*. New York: Harper and Row.

Krauss, R. 1945. *The Carrot Seed*. New York: Harper and Row.

Lexau, J. M. 1983. *Miss Harp in the Poison Ivy Case*. New York: Dial.

Linquist, W. 1970. *Stone Soup*. New York: Western.

Lionni, L. 1963. *Swimmy*. New York: Knopf.

Lobel, A. 1970. *Frog and Toad Are Friends*. New York: HarperCollins.

———. 1982. *Ming Lo Moves the Mountain*. New York: Greenwillow.

Mack, S. 1974. *Ten Bears in My Bed*. New York: Pantheon.

Mariana. 1962. *Miss Flora McFlimsey's Valentine*. New York: Lothrop, Lee and Shepard.

Marshall, J. 1989. *The Three Little Pigs*. New York: Dial Books for Young Readers.

Martin, B. 1967. *Brown Bear, Brown Bear, What Do You See?* New York: Holt.

McCloskey, R. 1948. *Blueberries for Sal*. New York: Viking.

———. 1957. *Time of Wonder*. New York: Puffin.

McGovern, A. 1967. *Too Much Noise*. Boston: Houghton Mifflin.

McNulty, F. 1979. *How to Dig a Hole to the Other Side of the World*. New York: Harper and Row.

Moore, E. 1964. *Johnny Appleseed*. New York: Scholastic.

Nimi, K., and K. Kuroi. 1986. *Gon Kitsune, a Fox Named Gon.* Tokyo: Kaisei-Sha.

Parish, P. 1963. *Amelia Bedelia.* New York: Harper and Row.

———. 1988. *Amelia Bedelia's Family Album.* New York: Greenwillow.

Perrault, C. 1954. *Cinderella.* New York: Scribner's.

———. 1983. *Little Red Riding Hood.* Mankato, MN: Creative Education.

Piatti, C. 1964. *The Happy Owls.* New York: Atheneum.

Piper, W. 1954. *The Little Engine That Could.* New York: Platt and Munk.

Potter, B. 1902. *The Tale of Peter Rabbit.* New York: Scholastic.

Raferty, K. 1989. *Kids Gardening.* Palo Alto, CA: Klutz Press.

Ranger Rick. Vienna, VA: National Wildlife Federation.

Rockwell, A. 1954. *The Three Little Pigs.* New York: Random House.

———. 1984. *The Three Bears and Fifteen Other Stories.* New York: Harper and Row.

Sendak, M. 1963. *Where the Wild Things Are.* New York: Harper and Row.

———. 1962. *Chicken Soup with Rice: A Book of Months.* New York: Harper and Row.

Seuss, Dr. 1960. *Green Eggs and Ham.* New York: Random House.

———. 1970. *Mr. Brown Can Moo! Can You?* New York: Random House.

———. 1957. *The Cat in the Hat.* New York: Putnam.

Shaw, C. G. 1947. *It Looked Like Spilt Milk.* New York: Viking.

Shone, V. 1991. *Wheels.* New York: Scholastic.

Slobodkina, E. 1974. *Caps for Sale.* Reading, MA: Addison Wesley.

Sobel, D. J. 1970. *Encyclopedia Brown.* Camden, NJ: T. Nelson.

Torbert, A. 1990. *Grandfather Tang's Story: A Tale Told with Tangrams.* New York: Crown.

Udry, J. M. 1956. *A Tree Is Nice.* New York: Harper and Row.

Wildsmith, B. 1963. *The Lion and the Rat.* New York: Franklin Watts.

Wilhelm, H. 1988. *Tyrone the Horrible.* New York: Scholastic.

Williams, V. B. 1986. *Cherries and Cherry Pits.* New York: Greenwillow.

Wither, C. 1966. *The Tale of the Black Cat.* New York: Holt.

Yolen, J. 1987. *Owl Moon.* New York: Philomel.

Zolotow, C. 1962. *Mister Rabbit and the Lovely Present.* New York: Harper and Row.

———. 1972. *William's Doll.* New York: Harper and Row.

Literature Circles

Voice and Choice in the Student-Centered Classroom
Harvey Daniels

Two potent ideas—independent reading and cooperative learning—come together in this practical and exciting book. Literature circles is a favorite teaching technique, and this book presents a particularly effective way of getting started, using temporary role sheets to create quick, successful implementation of student-led discussion groups. Harvey Daniels offers a variety of structures and procedures for managing literature circles over the long run, strategies which solidify and deepen the contribution which this special activity can make to balance the curriculum across grade levels.

Paperback • 216 pages • 1-57110-000-8

Literature Study Circles in a Multicultural Classroom

Katharine Davies Samway and Gail Whang

Teachers everywhere successfully use literature circles. Gail Whang tells her story of moving from basals to literature circles and why that decision was such a winner. In her inner-city classroom of "at-risk" students, she had found her language arts program didn't work. As bored and discouraged as her fifth/sixth graders, she explored alternatives to traditional methods and began to use literature study circles (LSCs) to engage students and help them develop their abilities to think and talk about issues in their lives. Her new strategy worked; the cooperative, dynamic elements of literature circles drew the students into books and reading.

Paperback • 168 pages • 1-57110-018-0

True Stories

Nonfiction Literacy in the Primary Classroom
Christine Duthie

As a committed user of children's literature in the classroom, Chris Duthie decided to use more nonfiction in her first-grade classroom and soon realized that simply making the books available and reading them aloud was not enough. She discovered ways to make nonfiction an integral part of her classroom so that it became an equal partner with fiction in both reading and writing workshops. In *True Stories* she describes how she drew on children's real-life experiences and existing knowledge to nurture that sense of wonder through nonfiction author studies, reading nonfiction Big Books, close concentration on the visual elements of texts, and reading and writing biography and autobiography. Writing out of her own classroom experience, she offers a wealth of dependable ideas and proven methods that you can put to work every day.

Paperback • 176 pages • 1-57110-026-1

A Stenhouse
IN PRACTICE ▶
Book

Taking Note

Improving Your Observational Notetaking
Brenda Miller Power

Teachers need to be keen observers and notetakers as they assess how students learn. This practical guide will show you how to dig your way through a mountain of paperwork and keep thoughtful records of student learning. In a breezy, down-to-earth style Brenda Power invites you to try new notetaking strategies and shows you how developing this modest skill can help you organize your work and make you more efficient.

In dozens of examples from teachers at all grade levels, Brenda offers helpful suggestions and strategies for everyone from the first-year teacher to the veteran classroom researcher. She takes you step-by-step through the process of examining existing notes, breaking old habits, managing time and materials so observations are possible, and coding notes for later use in assessment and research. Every chapter is packed with ideas and techniques you can use to become a cogent, skillful, and accurate notetaker who knows how to get organized, what to make note of, and how to find the time to write up your notes and assessments.

Paperback • 104 pages • 1-57110-035-0

Team Teaching

**Northern Nevada Writing Project
Teacher-Researcher Group**

Team teaching is a strategy that has been around for years, but creating teams needs careful thought in order to succeed. Chock-full of ideas and insights, *Team Teaching* discusses the social and personal implications of teaming, illuminating the process with first-person vignettes taken from the journals classroom teachers kept to record their experiences.

Based on their own stories and those of their colleagues/informants the authors discuss how and why team teaching succeeds, how to get started, what team teaching can and can't do, and how principals, parents, and students see team teaching. Appendixes include a checklist of team teacher issues, a parent survey on teaming, and materials for questions and discussion groups about team teaching.

Paperback • 120 pages • 1-57110-040-7

*For information
on all Stenhouse publications,
please write or call for a catalogue.*

Stenhouse Publishers
P.O. Box 360
York, ME 03909
1-800-988-9812